CHAMPAGNE
COCKTAILS

50 CORK-POPPING CONCOCTIONS & SCINTILLATING SPARKLERS

A.J. RATHBUN

THE HARVARD COMMON PRESS
BOSTON, MASSACHUSETTS

The Harvard Common Press
535 Albany Street
Boston, Massachusetts 02118
www.harvardcommonpress.com

Printed in China
Printed on acid-free paper

Library of Congress Cataloging-in-Publication Data
Rathbun, A. J. (Arthur John), 1969-
 Champagne cocktails : 50 cork-popping concoc-
tions and scintillating sparklers / A.J. Rathbun.
    p. cm.
 Includes index.
 ISBN 978-1-55832-426-8 (hardcover : alk. paper)
 1. Cocktails. 2. Sparkling wines. I. Title.
 TX951.R164 2010
 641.8'74--dc22

                    2009050015

Special bulk-order discounts are available on
this and other Harvard Common Press books.
Companies and organizations may purchase books
for premiums or resale, or may arrange a custom
edition, by contacting the Marketing Director at the
address above.

Book design by Laura Palese
Photographs by Jerry Errico
Food and drink styling by Brian Preston-Campbell
Author photographs by Natalie Fuller

10 9 8 7 6 5 4 3 2 1

CONTENTS

For Rebecca Staffel, for opening the bottle, and for
Michael Bourret, for keeping the drinks and food flowing

ACKNOWLEDGMENTS

To ensure that bubbles don't get flat throughout a whole book takes
much more than just one person, which is a darn good thing—drinking
is never as much fun alone. For all the help keeping those bubbles bubbling, I'd like to thank everyone who's ever shared a bottle of any kind
of sparkling wine with me, whether it was mixed with other ingredients
or sipped solo. Here's to you, the Champagne of drinking companions.
But I'd also like to send out a few specific thanks to those who helped
with this particular bottle (well, book of bottles, really), starting out
with Valerie Cimino, my wonderful editor, who makes my ramblings so
much crisper and whose devotion to the art of finer drinks (especially
those from Venice) can never be doubted. A jeroboam of thanks, also,
to the whole staff at The Harvard Common Press, who are an effervescent and helpful batch of book-loving folk.

Speaking of opening big bottles of thanks, a magnum of sparkling
wine should be opened for a great drink photographer, Jerry Errico.
Thanks also to the whole Errico team for their assistance. A grammati-
cal toast, too, to copy editor Jane Dornbusch, whose keen eye kept this
book from dribbling out onto the floor.

Of course, another round of bottles must be delivered to my
agent, Michael Bourret (the dedication just isn't enough), for his
continual aid, advice, and ability to answer nearly any question
from anywhere.

An extra double magnum (maybe two) of the imported stuff must be opened for a few more select folks as well, for their help above and beyond the removal of a cork. These fine friends and bar companions include those who were kind enough to lend me recipes for this book (a huge shout-out to pal and boy bar genius Andrew Bohrer); filmatic mad mastermind Brad Kosel (and his basketball league) and Brad's charming wife Christi and son Cash; my pals at The Lisa Ekus Group; Brad (not Bradley) Parsons for support and championing the cause; Leslie for the website aid; Mark for the biz advice; Ed and Jill, Jerm, Meg, and Beatrix for testing anything and everything (oh heck, really, thanks to the whole Ballard Progressive Institution and anyone who sometimes hangs out with it); anyone who's left a comment or come by the Spiked Punch blog at www.ajrathbun.com/blog; my family near and far; and, as always, you.

But the last and largest bottle of thanks (a bottle of Prosecco, I think, or maybe Lambrusco) goes to the family I see each and every lucky day, those nutty dogs Sookie and Rory (who keep eating all the leftover bottle corks) and my wife, Natalie. Thanks for never skipping a beat when I get the punch bowl down for testing late on a weekday, for not missing the space now taken up by those extra bottles of sparkling wine, and for being ready, at a moment's notice, to go open those bottles where they were actually filled.

INTRODUCTION

Aren't celebrations wonderful? There's nothing better than getting together with friends, family, beaus and belles, a single pal, coworkers, even people you met only a minute ago to talk happily, sing songs, dance, perhaps say a few silly things, and just be joyous on a certain day. Maybe it's a somewhat serious type of cheerful day with long-term ramifications, such as a wedding, or a glad day at the end of a long project or task (a retirement, even), or a night when you want to gather those closest to you to tell them how much better they make your moments, or a moonlit night with you and that special someone, remembering a day 12 years ago when you had that first kiss. These celebrations, big and small, constitute much of what keeps life from sliding into a mundane morass.

Champagne, and sparkling wines of all types, has always added an extra serving of terrificness to these moments. A sparkler automatically brings a nice but not overwhelming touch of elegance anywhere it's opened up. The lively nature of these drinks matches up so well with happy occasions, and the fact that the bubbles in the bottle, as everyone knows, don't last forever reminds us to enjoy these special days that much more. For all these reasons, it's a shame to have your wingdings, soirées, and generally festive fêtes without making sure old pal Champagne or one of her cousins is around in some form.

I think, too, that having a particular Champagne cocktail, or other sparkling mixed drink, makes the occasions even more spectacular.

Not that I don't enjoy a glass of plain Prosecco, mind you. But picking out a signature drink—one that really matches the big-or-small occasion, one that tastes great and mirrors the moment's personality—adds a touch of transformative magic that elevates an event into rollicking, memorable revelry. And isn't having memorable and exciting parties what throwing parties is all about? It isn't, after all, a party if it happens every night, and your drink should have that same "I'm special" kind of attitude. And Champagne cocktails certainly do.

The classic (and simply named) Champagne Cocktail, with its graceful mingling of sugar, Angostura bitters, and Champagne, has been around at least since the latter part of the 1800s and is featured in Jerry Thomas's *Bar-Tender's Guide* from 1862. And Mimosas and Bellinis have made it to brunch menus from Maine to California. But why stop with these (not that they aren't great)?

I say, uncork and start up the sparklers. Having a little gathering next week to celebrate turning 30? Try a Happy Youth to let folks know that age isn't going to change your outlook. Want to have a winter holiday hoedown that folks actually are happy to attend? Mention Bubbly Poinsettias on the invites and watch the RSVPs flow in. Or, just turn the pages, get your cabinets stocked, and delve into the effervescent world of the Sea Horse, Sweeter Welcome, Black Velvet, Buck's Fizz, and their cheerful and singular bubbly brothers and sisters. These beauties are sure to make those special days, big and small, spent with those closest to you, those days that make life worth living, even better.

1

The Bubbly
BASICS

WHEN TALKING ABOUT SPARKLING WINE,
the discussion starts with Champagne itself. And this is the way it
should be. However, to the detriment of both the real Champagne, the
genuine stuff, and the many other worthy sparkling wines available
worldwide, some bubblies that are called "Champagne" in passing
actually are not Champagne. So before the drinks start bubbling, let's
go over the basics.

CHAMPAGNE

The leader of the pack when it comes to lively wines, thanks in part to
its early identification with French royalty, Champagne is regal and
occasionally raucous, an automatic insertion of class into a room. It's
also selective, but not in any way that should stop you from drinking it.
To truly carry the name *Champagne*, by law and treaties and international signatures, the wine must be from the Champagne region
in France and made by inducing a secondary fermentation of a wine

using yeast and rock sugar inside the bottle (when sparkling wines in other places use this same technique, they can be said to use the *méthode champenoise* or *méthode traditionnelle*). This fermentation increases the level of carbon dioxide, which makes the wine bubble. Though some think Dom Pérignon (a seventeenth-century Benedictine monk) invented Champagne, he really just helped to advance production techniques, including developing the wire frame that holds the cork in place to keep *le vin du diable* (the "devil's wine," as it was once called because of the bubbles) from getting out too soon. The first sparkling wine, from what I've discovered, came from the Limoux area of the then Languedoc (now Languedoc-Roussillon) region of France in 1535.

There are five main sweetness levels of Champagne, from driest to sweetest: brut, extra-dry, sec, demi-sec, and doux, and the rest of the sparkling wine world has also adopted these classifications. Two other levels, brut natural and extra-brut, are not seen as often. Mostly what you'll discover in your local wine shop is of the brut or extra-dry variety, but if you can find the others, give 'em a whirl. Champagne tends to be made from the white Chardonnay grape or the darker-skinned Pinot Noir or Pinot Meunier grapes. Rosé Champagne is created by adding a little red wine during the blending process, or (more rarely) by letting the grape skins remain in contact with the juice.

OTHER FRENCH SPARKLING WINES

While Champagne gets most of the talk and lots of the props, there are other good sparkling wines made in France, mostly under the designation of Crémant. Crémant sparkling wines are named after the region they come from, and their production follows strict rules, including the use of grapes harvested by hand and an aging period of at least one year; they are also made using the traditional Champagne method. These can be both used in place of Champagne in mixed drinks and consumed on their own.

France also produces other sparkling wines—watch for the word *mousseux*, which means "sparkling" and which is used to call out sparkling French wines made by a different method (usually the Charmat method, which is when the bubbling process happens in stainless-steel fermentation tanks). These wines will tend toward lower price points and are well worth investigating.

ITALIAN SPARKLING WINES

Italy has a rich history of sparkling wines and a nice variety of flavors and personalities represented. The generic term for fully sparkling wines in Italy is *spumante*, which came into use around 1908 to refer to wines in the bubbly family. *Frizzante* is used to refer to wines with a lighter effervescence (the French equivalent is *pétillant*). Perhaps the best-known Italian sparkler is Prosecco. You can track down Prosecco in the less-sparkling *frizzante* style or in the bubblier *spumante* style. Most Prosecco comes from the Valdobbiadene region, but other regions produce it, too. It tends to be right between dry and sweet—a touch less dry than most sparkling wines, though you can get sweeter varieties as well (which pair so nicely with dessert), and you can find rosé Proseccos, too.

Slightly on the sweet side, Asti wines come from the province of the same name, and include *spumante* wines as well as *frizzante* wines, as well as the specially designated and delicious Moscato d'Asti. With their own designation and rules, and produced by the traditional Champagne method, Italian sparkling wines are cherished throughout the world.

Another well-known Italian sparkling wine, Trento, is also made by the traditional method, with both white and rosé varieties. There are two red *frizzante* Italian wines that turn up regularly, Brachetto and Lambrusco. The former tends to be a bit more bubbly and sweeter, and sometimes reaches *spumante* stage, while the latter is known for its very delicate fizz, which is like a little whisper on the tongue. Be sure when buying Lambrusco that you get *frizzante*, as some still wine is marketed under the same name.

OTHER EUROPEAN SPARKLING WINES

While French and Italian sparklers get a lot of the talk, both Spain and Germany make worthy sparkling varieties. In Spain, Cava is the sparkler, made in both white and rosé, following the traditional method; its history goes all the way back to 1872. You can find Cava in five levels of sweetness: brut nature, brut, seco, semiseco, and dulce. In Germany, sparkling wines are called Sekt. Nearly all Sekt is made by the Charmat process, with just a bit being made by the traditional method. Most contain wines imported from other European countries; only those bottles labeled *Deutscher Sekt* use solely German grapes. If you see a German sparkler called *Perlwein,* it wasn't made following Sekt's stricter guidelines (and also may not have the forceful bubbling for which Sekt is known). It's still perfectly quaffable, though.

AMERICAN SPARKLING WINES

America's a big country, and as might be expected, it produces many sparkling wines, made using both the Charmat method (usually for more mass-market offerings) and the traditional process (for higher-end wines). The first commercial American sparkling wines were made in California in 1892 by the Korbel brothers, but today, tasty sparkling wines, both white and rosé, are made in many states, including Washington, Oregon, New York, and others. While American sparkling wines tend to follow the traditional French sweetness scale, there aren't rules constraining specific levels, so it's never a bad idea to test a wine that's new to you to ensure you know what you're in for.

OTHER SPARKLING WINES

While the above covers a lot of the sparkling ground, there are many more sparkling wines being made worldwide. A couple of notables include Australian sparkling wines, created by both methods; don't overlook sparkling Shiraz, which is a red sparkler that can be sweet or dry but which tends to have a rich, frothy nature that makes it stand out—on the shelf (and on the palate). South Africa's Cap Classique sparkling wines, which are made by the traditional French method, tend to be dry and light and lovely on a spring afternoon. But there are more sparklers being produced in more places all the time, so keep in close touch with your wine seller, and don't stop the sparkling adventures.

SUBSTITUTING SPARKLING WINES IN THIS BOOK

As the above shows, there are many, many sparkling wines out there—leading to the question: Can various types and varieties be easily substituted in this book's recipes? The short answer: sometimes. For each recipe there is suggested either a level of sweetness, such as "brut" sparkling wine or Champagne, or a more specific type of sparkling wine, such as "Australian Shiraz." In the former situation, it is okay, for example, to use an American brut-style sparkling wine or a French brut-style sparkling wine (or any brut-style sparkling wine). There are going to be taste differences among the wines, but the basic sweetness level specified is what's going to work best in the drink; in other words, don't switch to an extra-dry in those recipes. In cases where specific types of sparkling wine are suggested, you should always stick to the type. If you substitute a brut-style sparkling wine for an Australian Shiraz in Eurynome's Effervescence (page 39), for example, it will completely alter the drink. If you're having problems finding a particular type of sparkling wine at your local store (and you really shouldn't have too much trouble), try online.

MAKE MY INGREDIENTS MERRY

There's no doubt who's the hero in the drinks within this book: the sparkling wines and Champagne family. But even the top superheroes need a little help from their sidekicks, and in the same way, the sparklers rise to new heights when combined with the right ingredients. This is why you'll want to get the rest of your bar stocked up.

LOVING LIQUORS AND LIQUEURS

Not all, but most, of the drinks in this book mix sparkling wine with one or more liquors or liqueurs. When purchasing gin, vodka, whiskey, rum, and so forth, remember that they are going to be mixed with bubbly and other ingredients. Go for good, midrange to upper-midrange bottles of liquors and you'll be set.

MIXING UP NICE WITH MANY MIXERS

The category of "mixers" is a broad one, but manageable when you remember one simple maxim: Fresh rules! This means that using fresh mixers results in better drinks. The spotlight gleams perhaps brightest on fruit juice. Many of the drinks in this book use juice, and those drinks taste tons better when that juice is freshly squeezed from ripe fruit. To get the most juice from your fruit, let it get to room temperature before using, or, in a pinch, wrap it in a damp towel and microwave it for about 20 seconds or run it under warm water, both of which will help get the juice flowing. You can also roll a piece of fruit under your palm with a steady pressure for a few seconds. The fresh rule also applies to things like club soda and ginger ale (be sure your bottled mixers have a hearty pizzazz when opened and not a lowly *pfhhhh*) and grenadine (I suggest Stirrings brand, or even making your own, as some store-bought varieties are a bit overly sweet) and almost any other mixer you'll find. The fresh rule goes for fruit, too, like pineapple: Please don't ever use canned fruit in your drinks.

Two mixers skirt around the fresh rule. The first is bitters. Bitters are flavoring agents that are crucial to many, many drinks. For a while in the twentieth century they seemed in danger of being forgotten. They've made a recent comeback, and drinks are better for them. Basically, bitters are collections of herbs, spices, and other goodies in liquid form, used in small amounts to add flavor, balance, and magic to drinks of various sorts and sizes. Bitters come in small bottles and can be stored in a cool, dry, place away from sunlight for a long period of time (though you'll probably use them often enough that they won't stick around *too* long). When a recipe calls for a specific type of bitters, you should use it (if you're having trouble finding a particular brand, look online). If you have to substitute a different one, the drink might still be tasty—but it'll be a different drink.

The second exception to the fresh rule is simple syrup (page 16), a sugar-and-water combination that's a snap to make. It's used in enough of the following pages' effervescent beauties that I suggest always having a bottle of simple syrup around. Once you've made it, store it, well sealed, in the refrigerator for up to a month.

GLITTERING (AND GOOD-TASTING) ICE

Many of these drinks use cold sparkling wine to chill out, but a lot also use ice, and what ice brings to a drink is crucial. With a few ice niceties in mind, you'll achieve a high level of beverage brilliance. First, most calls for ice here (outside of the punch chapter) are of the regular 1-inch ice cube variety. But remember, fresh rules. You want to avoid old ice that's been getting too friendly in the freezer with the fish you caught last summer, because the ice will take on the flavors of nearby foods. If you don't have any ice cubes, buy cracked ice and use it instead (though remember that cracked ice, due to its irregular shapes, melts a little

SIMPLE SYRUP Makes about 4½ cups

2½ CUPS WATER

3 CUPS SUGAR

1   *Combine the water and sugar in a medium-size saucepan. Stirring occasionally, bring the mixture to a boil over medium-high heat. Lower the heat a bit, keeping the mixture at a low boil for 5 minutes.*

2   *Turn off the heat, and let the syrup cool completely in the pan. Store in an airtight container in the refrigerator for up to 1 month.*

faster). For punches, I think it's cool (on many levels) to use a block of ice or an ice ring in your punch bowl. Ice blocks can be bought in stores, or you can make your own with a bundt cake pan or other ring mold.

GARNISHES ARE MORE THAN EFFERVESCENCE FOR THE EYE

It's the little touches that turn an everyday affair into a legendary celebration that's talked about in respectful tones for years afterward. In the same way, it's the garnish that often takes drinks from ho-hum (or even a few steps above) to holy-cow-that's-amazing. Garnishes not only serve as a drink's visual *pièce de résistance*, an accessory that makes the outfit, they add vital flavor notes. It should nearly go without saying that with garnishes, as with mixers, fresh rules!

The citrus garnish family needs an in-depth overview, because its members play in different ways when in different drinks, and it's necessary to know the various forms and how to make those forms. I'm talking about citrus twists, wheels, and wedges. The first type, twists, may perhaps be the trickiest. Sadly, twists are also the most underutilized. Though they look nice, their true function is to release the essential oils in the fruit's rind into a drink. These oils are super-fragrant and luscious, so if you see a twist just draped over a drink and not twisted into it, or if you see a bartender peeling them off a fruit nowhere near the drink, letting the oils escape into the air, don't be shy about crying. The saddest part may be that it's not hard to make a useful and attractive twist. Begin by cutting off the bottom end of a citrus fruit in a straight line. You don't need to cut too much off, but you do want a flat surface. Then, place your fruit, cut side down, on a cutting board. With a sharp knife, cut ½-inch-wide strips of peel from top to bottom. Try to get as little of the fruit's white pith as possible while maintaining good, wide pieces of peel. The strips of peel are your twists, which you want to be able to twist over the top of a drink without having them break.

The next garnish types are wheels, half-wheels or slices, and wedges, and all are easy-peasy to whip out. The first two start by slicing off the ends of your fruit with your friendly knife. Then, slice the fruit into wheels (⅛ to ¼ inch thick); cut the wheels in half for slices. If you're going to perch them on a glass's edge when serving, cut notches in them. To make wedges, start the same way, cutting the ends off your fruit. Next, cut the fruit in half lengthwise, and then lay each half, cut side down, on your cutting board. Make three top-to-bottom cuts in each half, leaving three equal-size pieces. Cut those pieces in half crosswise for small to medium-size fruits, and in thirds for large fruits. Sometimes folks call these small pieces "quarters" and the large pieces "wedges," which is fine. But for this book, let's stick with calling those smaller pieces wedges, so we stay on the same bubble.

THE TWINKLE OF TRUE GLASSWARE

Before getting into the types of glassware you'll want, I need to put down a salient point: Glass is always better than plastic, especially when you're filling the vessels with a sparkling mix.

Luckily, you can invest in a few choice glasses and be ready to roll (or shake and strain, as the case may be) without breaking the proverbial bank. The first type of glass that you'll want twinkling on your shelf is a flute glass. Flutes are known for their tall and narrow bowls and, usually, long stems. This design helps contain the carbonation by reducing the available surface area (more surface area on the top of the drink means it's easier for those bubbles to bubble out). This keeps your sparklers sparkling, which isn't a bad thing. I would suggest at least a set of six, and you may want to invest in more for larger affairs. Flutes range in size from 6 to 9 ounces, but be careful—if you get one that's very large, go on the lean side when a drink's instructions tell you to top it off with sparkling wine. In general, "topping it off" should involve no more than 4 ounces.

While the flute rules today, for many years bubbly and bubbly cocktails were served in the wider-mouthed Champagne coupe or Champagne saucer, which looks a bit like a cocktail glass (a.k.a. a martini glass), but with a more curved bowl. This glass does let that carbonation escape a little more than a flute does, but it also has a lovely appearance, and the way the effervescence plays across the wider bowl is elegant and adds a touch of *je ne sais quoi* to certain late-night occasions. If you can't track any down, I suggest picking up a set of regulation-size cocktail glasses, in the 6- to 10-ounce range.

The crucial glassware for most of the recipes in the last chapter is a punch bowl. Punch bowls are readily available at many kitchenware stores, both online and off, as well as at antiques shops. To go with your punch bowl, you'll want some punch glasses (many bowls come with glasses—an excellent package deal). Punch glasses tend to be on the smallish side. If you can't lay your hands on cute punch glasses, then use white wine glasses or red wine goblets; I'll bet you won't get any complaints. For that matter, picking up a set of both kinds of wine glasses is a good idea, as they are used for certain drinks in this book.

TERRIFIC TOOLS SPARKLE IN TURN

While ingredients are key, and glassware is essential, there are some drink-making tools that you'll find indispensable when whipping up sparkling cocktails. And at the head of that tool list is the cocktail shaker. There are two kinds available, and both deliver great results and well-chilled drinks. The first is the Boston shaker, which has two cups: a glass bottom cup and a metal top cup. You will also need a bar strainer for this type of shaker. It might take a minute to get the swing of using it, but it's not really hard. You begin by adding ice and ingredients to the glass cup. Then, place the metal top cup over that bottom cup and, holding the bottom with one hand, carefully give the top cup a little thump with your other hand to create a seal between the two pieces. Flip the whole thing over, being sure to hold both pieces securely, and shake the drink (which is now in the metal cup). Then place the shaker on a flat surface, metal side down, and carefully strike or nudge the metal piece to break the seal. Strain, garnish, and you're good to go.

The cobbler shaker, our second shaker type, has a bigger bottom piece that's covered by a smaller top piece that fits into the bottom. The top piece tends to have a built-in strainer and cap (which can often be used to measure ingredients). Add your ice and ingredients to the bottom piece, secure the top piece in the bottom piece, and then shake it up. Remove that top cap, strain, garnish, and serve.

Whichever cocktail shaker you decide on, be sure to pick one that has 18/10 stainless steel pieces and feels good in your hands. Most drinks should be shaken for about 10 seconds (unless instructions say otherwise), and so you'll want to be comfortable.

While the cocktail shaker stands tall (literally and figuratively) on the bar tool shelf, there are some other crucial friends you'll want to be sure to have around, starting with at least one measuring device. I suggest getting a solid stainless steel jigger, one with a 1-ounce measurement mark on one side and a 2-ounce one on the other, or one that has ½-ounce and 1½-ounce marks. Another tool that comes in handy on a regular basis is a muddler, for knocking fruit or herbs around a bit in your cocktail shaker, both to get the juice out and to release flavors that reside in rinds and leaves.

Other tools that you'll probably use on a regular basis include a large pitcher, a sharp garnishing knife, and a juicer of some kind (either a handheld juice squeezer, a lever model juicer, or a motorized juice extractor). A long, thin, attractive (because you want to look good when making the drinks) stirring spoon is also going to be a big boon, as you'll often be stirring ingredients into the sparkling wine.

A FINAL WORD

You've gotten your bubbly basics, stocked up the bar a bit, lined some shelves with good glasses and tools, and are about to enter the realm of the Champagne cocktail. I don't want to stall your celebration, but there is one final ingredient that should never be forgotten when making these drinks: fun. Having fun while sipping with friends and family is the key to success. Even with the finest fizzy drink, if you're not having fun, well, you've forgotten a vital part of the whole experience. Having said that, there's nothing left but to turn the page and become a part of the Champagne cocktail cosmos—a mighty fine place to be.

2

The Carbonated
CLASSICS

GET READY FOR THE HEAVY HITTERS, THE LOOMING
liquid texts, the serious (if sparkling) drinks, the hallowed mixes, the
classics. Isn't it sad how we deem things *classic* and then shuffle them
off as dusty, replacing them with fly-by-nights? Reverse the trend with
the following drinks, which are as lively today as the day they were created and which are masterpieces not because they require serious study
to be enjoyed but solely because their great taste goes well in any era.

Champagne Cobbler
Bellini
Champagne Bowler
Black Velvet

Champagne Cocktail
French 75
Kir Royale
Her Sarong Slipped

Death in the Afternoon
Seelbach Cocktail
Mimosa

CHAMPAGNE COBBLER

The Champagne Cobbler (like the paterfamilias of this book, the Champagne Cocktail, on page 26) traces itself back to the cocktail and drink craze of the middle to late 1800s. The big hit of the cobbler family at the time was the Sherry Cobbler, but there were many variations, including this merry one. "The Professor" Jerry Thomas has a Champagne Cobbler recipe in his 1862 *Bar-Tender's Guide*, and I don't stray too far from it. He used shaved ice, and I suggest you do the same, but if you can't, go with crushed ice. If you can ornament with berries in the manner Mr. Thomas suggests, that'd be a rollicking time, but I like mint leaves as well. He also goes with lemon and orange pieces, and you could, too. (Sometimes I use straight orange, but that's just 'cause I sometimes run out of lemons.)   SERVES 4

CRUSHED ICE

6 OUNCES SIMPLE SYRUP *(page 16)*

CHILLED BRUT CHAMPAGNE

4 ORANGE TWISTS *for garnish*

4 LEMON TWISTS *for garnish (optional)*

FRESH MINT LEAVES *for garnish (optional)*

BERRIES OF YOUR CHOICE *(blue-, rasp-, or black- all work nicely) for garnish*

1   *Fill four goblets three-quarters full with crushed ice. Add 1½ ounces simple syrup to each glass, then fill almost to the top with Champagne.*

2   *Twist an orange twist and a lemon twist, if using, over each glass, and then drop them into said glass. Stir well. Garnish with the mint, if using, and the berries, and serve.*

A VARIATION: In his excellent book about Jerry Thomas, *Imbibe!* (Perigee, 2007), cocktail historian David Wondrich says that "this is a nice one to make with a rosé Champagne." Now, that's thinking.

Champagne Cobbler photo page 1

BELLINI

The Bellini may come in second only to the Champagne Cocktail (page 26) in the delicious race to be called a true "classic" Champagne mixed drink. The Kir Royale might quibble a bit, and the Mimosa may wake up earlier, but the Bellini is known in so many far-flung and romantic corner tables of the world that I think it deserves the red ribbon.

The story goes that the name traces its history to a fifteenth-century painter, Jacopo Bellini, known for a "pink glow" in his paintings, echoed nicely by the glow of the drink. At least, that's what Harry Cipriani, bartender at Harry's Bar, thought when he mixed up the first one in 1948. Remember old Harry and Venice and Jacopo and art the next time you have a Bellini, and you'll be better for it. You'll also be better if you can use white peaches in your puree, along with a bit of lemon juice (a trick I learned from cocktail genius Gary Regan), and always use the Italian sparkling wine Prosecco. SERVES 2

2 WHITE PEACHES, *pitted*

ICE CUBES

½ OUNCE FRESHLY SQUEEZED LEMON JUICE

8 OUNCES PROSECCO

1 *Put the peach flesh and skin, one or two ice cubes, and the lemon juice in a blender. Blend until you have a smooth puree.*

2 *Pour 2 ounces of the precious puree into each of two flute glasses. Slowly, stirring gently with a long spoon, add 4 ounces of Prosecco to each glass. Serve immediately.*

A NOTE: You can also track down white peach puree at www.perfectpuree.com.

"They were disappointed beyond measure when the plebe-ian drunks decided to take it as a joke; they played red-dog and twenty-one and jack-pot from dinner to dawn, and on the occasion of one man's birthday persuaded him to buy sufficient champagne for a hilarious celebration."
—F. SCOTT FITZGERALD, *THIS SIDE OF PARADISE*, 1920

CHAMPAGNE BOWLER

Dating back at least to 1941, the Champagne Bowler isn't what you might think of as a "classic" when surrounded by some of its more renowned siblings. Let's call it an undiscovered classic, then (or at least I'm calling it that—you can make *tut-tut* noises and agitate your head disapprovingly in the corner, or you can come out and have a drink). It's a first-class ticket for affairs where you wear the hat in the drink's name, the kind of entertainments where you might refer to Champagne as "the boy" (which, seriously, they used to do back in England in days gone by).   SERVES 2

6 OR 7 STRAWBERRIES

2 OUNCES SIMPLE SYRUP *(page 16)*

ICE CUBES

2 OUNCES WHITE WINE

1 OUNCE COGNAC

8 OUNCES CHILLED BRUT SPARKLING WINE

1   *Place the strawberries and simple syrup within your finest cocktail shaker. Using a muddler, sturdy wooden spoon, or tiny umbrella, muddle well.*

2   *Fill the cocktail shaker halfway full with ice cubes. Add the white wine and Cognac and shake well.*

3   *Strain the mixture into two goblets or, if no goblets are lying around, red wine glasses. Top each with 4 ounces of the sparkling wine, stir briefly, and serve with a slight nod.*

BLACK VELVET

If you can make me a round of well-proportioned Black Velvets while singing the immortal Kiss song "Black Diamond," I will buy you the next round of your choice. If you can do it while wearing thigh-high boots sporting dragon-head soles, I'll buy the next two rounds.

I've seen the Black Velvet (which has also been called the Bismarck, after a German chancellor who was fond of them) made with varying proportions (using less or more stout), but I like it half-and-half. If that's too stouty for your tastes, pull back a bit on the dark stuff, and bring your sparkling wine or Champagne side to bear. Classically, this would be made with actual Champagne, to speak to the plush nature of the name and drink. But I think since the mix is half stout, using another good sparkling wine is okay. What isn't okay is not making this for a group. It goes so well with more than one, and also uses the beer better. **SERVES 4 (OR GENE, PETER, PAUL, AND ACE)**

TWO 12-OUNCE BOTTLES OF COLD STOUT *or other dark beer*
24 OUNCES CHILLED BRUT CHAMPAGNE *or other sparkling wine*

1   *Pour 6 ounces of stout into each of four glittering 12-ounce beer glasses or other 12-ounce glasses.*

2   *Add 6 ounces of Champagne to each of the glasses. Stir once, and no more. Serve immediately.*

CHAMPAGNE COCKTAIL

If you want to trace the word *sparkle* back to the Old Norse *sparkr*, I certainly won't peep about it. Or, if you go back to the Old English *spearca*, and want to deliver a point, I'll follow your point and even read the footnotes. If you, perhaps, would rather contend that this sparkling drink was once shaken a bit and so should be today, I'll listen calmly to your arguments and nod reflectively, even if I do disagree. If you'd rather, while reclining in two large chairs, posit that Peychaud's or Angostura bitters or your very own house bitters goes better than orange bitters in this, I'll weigh out each possibility, one glass at a time, while you state your liquid position. Truth be told, I'll be happy to contemplate any of your talking points on this simple and simply delicious classic, as long as you don't let my glass run dry.   SERVES 2

2 SUGAR CUBES

6 DASHES ORANGE BITTERS

CHILLED BRUT CHAMPAGNE

2 LEMON TWISTS *for garnish*

1   *Add a sugar cube to each of two flute glasses in any manner you see fit. Dash 3 dashes of orange bitters over each cube. Let them settle in for a minute.*

2   *Fill the flutes almost to the top with Champagne. Garnish each with a lemon twist and serve immediately.*

A VARIATION: As mentioned above, it can be rather fun to switch around your bitters in this elegant equation. Both Angostura and Peychaud's do nice things to the end result. And your homemade bitters (if you have them) probably are swell, too.

A SECOND VARIATION: As my elegant pal Valerie once mentioned, making this with a rosé Champagne is also a classic move, and darn swell, too. I suggest you give it a whirl.

FRENCH 75

Raise your glasses in a cheer, *mon ami*, to Claude Joseph Rouget de Lisle of Strasbourg, who might have toyed with the lines "You drinkers of French 75s, shake to glory, / Hark, hark! what bubbling flutes you raise!" before coming up with the current lines of the French national anthem "La Marseillaise." He knew this *gracieux* sparkler would rise back into popularity (after a bit of time spent mostly unsipped in the backs of recipe books and buried under lore and legend, like too many great drinks) and onto menus of bars. So bring strong voices into song when lifting glasses in reverence to our French songsmith (and maybe this loud toasting will keep him, wherever he is, from batting a spiritual eye at my small change to his lyrics).   SERVES 2

ICE CUBES

2 OUNCES GIN

1 OUNCE FRESHLY SQUEEZED LEMON JUICE

1 OUNCE SIMPLE SYRUP *(page 16)*

CHILLED BRUT CHAMPAGNE *or sparkling wine*

2 LEMON SLICES

2 ORANGE SLICES *for garnish (optional)*

2 MARASCHINO CHERRIES *for garnish (optional)*

1   *Add one or two ice cubes to each of two flute glasses. Add 1 ounce gin, ½ ounce lemon juice, and ½ ounce simple syrup to each glass. Stir happily.*

2   *Top off each flute with Champagne and a lemon slice. Garnish each with an orange and cherry if you're feeling like a fruit salad. Serve.*

A NOTE: If your sparkling wine is well chilled, feel free to omit the ice cubes. But this one should be cold.

A VARIATION: The way I've heard it, if you sub in brandy or Cognac for gin, it's a French 76. Some think this is just a pacifying flip for those who believe the French 75 was named for France (it was actually named for a big gun used in World War I).

KIR ROYALE

Doesn't this regal moniker make you wish you ran a fizzy town in France, where you'd serve a drink such as this to visiting potentates, who would then capitulate to your demands since they'd be so impressed with the drink? Well, this is just what Felix Kir, the mayor of Dijon, France, did back in the middle part of last century. Though, admittedly, he first used white wine mixed usually (the story goes) with crème de cassis, a black-currant liqueur, so that drink is called a Kir. Adding the bubbly "royale," though, gives it extra regality, and using framboise (a French raspberry-flavored brandy, not to be confused with the Belgian fruit beer of the same name) adds a nice flavor burst. Either liqueur (or Chambord, made from French black raspberries—another choice often seen here) results in a drink that rules.

SERVES 4

4 OUNCES FRAMBOISE

CHILLED BRUT CHAMPAGNE

4 LEMON TWISTS *for garnish*

1   *Pour 1 ounce of framboise into each of four flute glasses. Fill each flute with the chilled Champagne.*

2   *Twist a twist over each drink, drop it in, and make the pronouncement to start drinking.*

"He said not a word, but came painfully to the table, and made a motion towards the wine. The Editor filled a glass of champagne, and pushed it towards him. He drained it, and it seemed to do him good: for he looked round the table, and the ghost of his old smile flickered across his face."
—H.G. WELLS, *THE TIME MACHINE*, 1895

HER SARONG SLIPPED

All right, all right, don't get your underpants in a bunch—I understand that you don't know (or barely know, or have only heard of in whispers) this coquettish and smooth number, and so how can it possibly have made the massive move to masterpiece? Well, these things (like love, often) take time, cuties. With its teasing brandy, lemon, and sweet flavors sharing a liquid dalliance on a bubbly bed (whew, is it hot in here?), and that single strawberry slice waiting to be popped into the mouth—are you going to tell this long, tall lovely that it isn't a classic? Or are you going to make it your mission to help spread the love? I see you as the latter.   SERVES 2

ICE CUBES

3 OUNCES BRANDY

1 OUNCE FRESHLY SQUEEZED LEMON JUICE

½ OUNCE GRENADINE

CHILLED BRUT CHAMPAGNE *or sparkling wine*

2 STRAWBERRY SLICES *for garnish*

1   *Fill a cocktail shaker halfway full with ice cubes. Add the brandy, lemon juice, and grenadine. Shake, and put your hips into it.*

2   *Strain into two white wine glasses, and top each with Champagne. Garnish with the strawberry slices and serve with a wink.*

A NOTE: You ask if this needs to be served while wearing an actual sarong? I think you know the answer already.

A VARIATION: This also plays well with others when made with a sparkling rosé.

DEATH IN THE AFTERNOON

Though some know him more for his love of Daiquiris and Moji-tos, tough-guy writer Ernest Hemingway also maintained a love of absinthe, drinking it during his time in France and then later in Cuba and Florida (the story goes that he brought it in from Cuba, as it was illegal in this country at the time). He celebrated it so much that it was the main character's favorite in his novel *For Whom the Bell Tolls*, and then he contributed the recipe for this drink to a 1935 collection of celebrity recipes (naming it after his bullfighting novel—but no animal acts are needed when consuming it). However, that's just the entertainment news: The other story is that this minimal and elegant mixture is a fine sipper to have when the sunlight's winding down for the day.

SERVES 4

6 OUNCES ABSINTHE *(see A Note)*

16 OUNCES CHILLED CAVA *or other sparkling wine*

Divide the absinthe among four flute glasses. Top each with about 4 ounces of the sparkling wine. Serve immediately.

A NOTE: Absinthe, thankfully, is now readily available. If you can't find it, try a pastis, such as Ricard or Pernod. But you may have Hemingway's ghost come a-haunting.

A SECOND NOTE: I suggest Cava here as a shout-out to Spain, which Hemingway loved. If you can't find it, try another good sparkling wine.

SEELBACH COCKTAIL

The Seelbach is another worthy mix that teeters on the edge of that not-as-well-known-as-it-should-be crevasse. It was served predominantly in the pre-Prohibition era, first at the Seelbach Hotel in Louisville, Kentucky; it was rediscovered by Adam Seger, the hotel's restaurant director, in 1995. Initially, he wouldn't release the recipe, until sweet-talking cocktail historians Gary and Mardee Haidin Regan convinced him that the drink would take on more mythological proportions, and be consumed by many more consumers, if the recipe were divulged. And so it was, first in their great book *New Classic Cocktails* (Macmillan, 1997) and later in Ted "Dr. Cocktail" Haigh's also great *Vintage Spirits and Forgotten Cocktails* (Quarry, 2004). It was from the latter that I picked up the idea of using Cointreau as opposed to just any triple sec. Both books suggest using Old Forester bourbon, and I, for one, recommend you follow their advice. SERVES 2

2 OUNCES BOURBON

1 OUNCE COINTREAU

14 DASHES PEYCHAUD'S BITTERS

14 DASHES ANGOSTURA BITTERS

CHILLED BRUT CHAMPAGNE *or sparkling wine*

2 ORANGE TWISTS *for garnish*

1   *Divide the bourbon, Cointreau, and the two bitters between two flute glasses. Stir briefly.*

2   *Fill the flutes almost to the top with the chilled Champagne. Stir again, but don't get nutty about it. Garnish with the orange twists and serve.*

A VARIATION: Far be it from me to veer off a memorable mix such as this, but in a pinch I once used a lemon twist, and I liked it quite a bit.

MIMOSA

Why, oh why, isn't there a song about the Mimosa? Something with just a trace of the blues living in it, but still a morning song (since the Mimosa is not only my brunch favorite—sorry, Mr. Bloody Mary—but many other folks' as well and, for that matter, has orange juice as a major component, making it a healthy way to start the day). Something like this: "But c'mon, c'mon on, bubbly Mimosa / C'mon, sparkly drink, we're begging you, / C'mon, c'mon down, you have OJ in you / Got to squeeze that juice right off the fruit." Now, something like that is a fitting tribute to this early morning *tour de force*. If you want to write your own Mimosa song, I say get started. Then video yourself, put it online, and send it to me.   SERVES 4

4 OUNCES FRESHLY SQUEEZED ORANGE JUICE *(see A Note)*

CHILLED BRUT CHAMPAGNE *or sparkling wine*

4 ORANGE SLICES *for garnish*

Divide the orange juice rhythmically among four flute glasses. Fill each glass with the Champagne. Garnish each with an orange slice and serve.

....

A NOTE: I'm sure we've all had many Mimosas made with OJ from a carton. Though I may have already said so, let me say it again, loudly: Fresh juice is so much better. Stick to fresh, and folks will be writing songs about you.

"Darling, would you run out and buy a bottle of Champagne?
I can't entertain as shabbily as this and I've spent everything
I have just buying vulgar things like Scotch and gin. I daren't
even cash another check."
—VIRGINIA ROWANS, *HOUSE PARTY*, 1954

3

The FRUIT and the FIZZ

CHAMPAGNE AND SPARKLING WINES GO WITH
fruit and fruity ingredients a touch better even than kicking back on
the deck with friends goes with a Sunday afternoon in May, when that
sun's shining true and bright for the first time in months. This fruit and
sparkler simpatico does make good sense—they are, after all, related
(don't forget that it's grapes that make delicious sparkling wines possible). Naturally, the friends, the deck, the sun, and the fruity bubbly
drinks go together, all together, the best of all.

HAPPY YOUTH

The point to remember, as you tipple off into the years past what one can call "youth," is that even if those joints are creaking, it's more of a roll than a jump out of bed, and staying up past midnight seems superheroic—even then, you can still capture that happy youth feeling by being silly, laughing it up, wearing a feather boa and not caring a hoot what anyone thinks, having the posse over for a series of pictures with fake mustaches, and always remembering that "youth" isn't, after all, a term stuck to a specific date, but rather one attached to a specific state of mind. Having a few Happy Youths doesn't hurt, either, when remembering how fun it is to be young. **SERVES 4**

ICE CUBES

6 OUNCES FRESHLY SQUEEZED ORANGE JUICE

4 OUNCES CHERRY HEERING

2 OUNCES SIMPLE SYRUP *(page 16)*

CHILLED EXTRA-DRY ROSÉ SPARKLING WINE *(see A Note)*

1   *Fill a cocktail shaker halfway full with ice cubes. Add the orange juice, the Cherry Heering, and the simple syrup. Shake youthfully.*

2   *Strain the mixture into four flute glasses. Top each with the sparkling wine and serve.*

· ·

A NOTE: I like the just-a-tad-less-dry-than-brut extra-dry rosé here, but it sure wouldn't be bad with brut sparkling wine (even non-rosé) either. I think the rosé is awfully youthful, though.

"Colouring her argument, she touched upon the occasion of the birth: cherry brandy poured in the kitchen at a quarter past eleven at night, she herself clapping her hands, then clasping them to give thanks."
—WILLIAM TREVOR, *DEATH IN SUMMER*, 1999

BUCK'S FIZZ

Be gentle with me (hey, I'm testing and testing these sparkling drinks for *you*, which means I deserve a touch of gentleness), but for years I thought of the Buck's Fizz as a slightly-less-orange-juiced Mimosa (page 34) originating in London at the early part of the last century. But who can blame me, when books such as *Chesterfield Cocktails*, by Anthony Hogg, published in the U.K. in 1979 and depicting a gentleman in an out-of-sight white-pants-and-shirt-and-baby-blue-jacketed suit, lists it as such? Luckily, Robert Hess (a.k.a. DrinkBoy), author of *The Essential Bartender's Guide* (Mud Puddle Books, 2008), cleared the waters and introduced us to the original version—bringing the Buck's Fizz out of the shadow of the Mimosa and giving it a little spotlight of its own. SERVES 2

4 OUNCES FRESHLY SQUEEZED ORANGE JUICE

2 DASHES CHERRY BRANDY

½ OUNCE GIN

8 OUNCES CHILLED BRUT SPARKLING WINE

2 ORANGE WEDGES *for garnish*

1   *Pour 2 ounces orange juice, 1 dash brandy, and ¼ ounce gin into each of two flute glasses, in that order and none other.*

2   *Pour 4 ounces of the sparkling wine slowly into each glass. Garnish each with an orange wedge and serve.*

A VIRGIN VARIATION: Want one for non-imbibers? Take out the gin and brandy and sub in ginger ale for the sparkling wine, and you'll be having a Buck's Nursery Fizz.

EURYNOME'S
EFFERVESCENCE

Say you're on an ocean beach, and up from the water sprouts a mermaid-esque lady. She's terrifically lovely and regal and has a gleam in her eyes that, if you don't mind me getting a bit flowery in speech, mirrors a star. You'd be struck a little speechless, I'm guessing, but luckily she's chatty, and says she's an Oceanid, a genuine daughter of the ocean, and listening to you and your pals cavorting has made her awfully thirsty for something besides H_2O, and she smiles as she says it, longing a little for an ordinary life where beach parties happen. You, of course, want to serve her the perfect drink. And now you have the ideal liquid arrangement for this moment.   **SERVES 2**

10 FRESH MINT LEAVES

1 OUNCE FRESH PINEAPPLE JUICE

ICE CUBES

3 OUNCES DARK RUM

2 OUNCES RHUM CLÉMENT CRÉOLE SHRUBB (see A Note)

8 OUNCES CHILLED SPARKLING AUSTRALIAN SHIRAZ

1   *Place 8 of the mint leaves and the pineapple juice in a cocktail shaker. Using a muddler, wooden spoon, or small trident, muddle carefully but well.*

2   *Fill the cocktail shaker halfway full with ice cubes. Add the rum and Créole Shrubb. Shake well.*

3   *Strain the mixture into two cocktail glasses or coupe glasses. Top each with 4 ounces of the sparkling Shiraz. Float 1 mint leaf on top of each glass and serve.*

....

A NOTE: Rhum Clément Créole Shrubb is an orange liqueur made in Martinique from orange peels, rum, and sugarcane syrup. It's becoming more readily available, but if you're having problems tracking it down, try online.

TIZIANO

While sailing the seven seas of drink lore one afternoon, I discovered this fizzer in Rob Chirico's handy *Field Guide to Cocktails* (Quirk, 2005), a volume chock-a-block with merriment, recipes, and solid advice, all in a book that could fit in the front pocket of a buccaneer's coat (or any large coat, I suppose). Tracing a fairly simple map to tastiness, the Tiziano is a cousin of the Bellini (page 23) that still forges ahead with its own identity. And that is an identity born out of white grape juice, so be sure you get a brand you know you can trust.

SERVES 4

6 OUNCES WHITE GRAPE JUICE

CHILLED PROSECCO

FROZEN GREEN OR RED GRAPES *for garnish*

1   *Pour 1½ ounces of the grape juice into each of four flute glasses.*

2   *Fill the glasses almost to the top with Prosecco. Carefully drop one or two grapes into each glass and serve.*

. . . .

A VARIATION: Change the white grape juice to strawberry juice or strawberry puree and garnish with a fresh (not frozen) strawberry instead of a grape, and you'll be drinking a Rossini, which is worthy of cheers, too.

ITALIAN DREAM

When you're having your very own Italian Dream (and everyone must have one, at least once), do you dream of a Renaissance castle on a mountain overlooking the Mar Tirreno, or of villas tucked away on rolling hillsides dotted with olive groves, or of historic apartments perched over high-fashion streets, or of just a single table outside a café where you can nurse a cappuccino and while away the hours watching people walk from masterpiece to masterpiece? Or do you dream of all of the above, plus wandering into a bookstore on a small side street and finding a handy manual called *Cocktail: Classici & Esotici*, which will have a drink in it called the Italian Dream, a tall *bella bevanda frizzante*? That, friends, is a dream that can come true.
SERVES 4

4 OUNCES AMARETTO

4 OUNCES FRESHLY SQUEEZED ORANGE JUICE

CHILLED ASTI SPUMANTE *(see A Note)*

4 MARASCHINO CHERRIES *for garnish*

1   *Place 1 ounce amaretto and 1 ounce orange juice into each of four flute glasses. Stir briefly.*

2   *Fill the flutes almost to the top with the Asti Spumante. Gently drop the cherries into the glasses and serve.*

....

A NOTE: Asti Spumante is a sparkling white wine from just south of Asti, a town in Italy's Piedmont region. It boasts a sweetness that comes from the specific filtration and fermentation process used to make the wine.

SOYER AU CHAMPAGNE

This silky, ice-creamy reverie should be served at festive dessert fêtes, accompanied by French accents, large white hats (for both sexes), either short flapper skirts and seersucker suits or flowing floral numbers and pressed trousers and spats, and oodles of cookies, some candies, and a heaping helping of chocolate mousse. The talk must center around how tennis is better on grass, how cheese is better when stinkier, and how Ted "Dr. Cocktail" Haigh's *Vintage Spirits and Forgotten Cocktails* (Quarry, 2004) is quite the place to flip the pages when wanting to find a fizzy vision from around 1888 to match up with such a soirée.   SERVES 2

4 DASHES MARASCHINO LIQUEUR

4 DASHES FRESH PINEAPPLE JUICE

4 DASHES GRAND MARNIER

4 DASHES BRANDY

CHILLED BRUT CHAMPAGNE

2 SCOOPS VANILLA ICE CREAM

1   *Add 2 dashes maraschino, 2 dashes pineapple juice, 2 dashes Grand Marnier, and 2 dashes brandy to each of two parfait glasses (see A Note). Stir each briefly.*

2   *Top the glasses off with Champagne, filling them almost to the top. Carefully add a scoop of ice cream to each glass. Haigh's suggestion is to serve with a straw and a spoon, which seems like the right tactic.*

A NOTE: A parfait glass is an elegant glass with a bit of a wide brim, originally created for drinks like this, with liquids and ice cream. They used to be 4 ounces (or thereabouts) but now are wider-ranging in size. You can find them in restaurant supply stores, antiques stores, and online, but if you can't track any down, try this in a white wine glass that's large enough to fit a spoon.

VALENTINE'S SLUMBER

Give it a rest, Romeo. Take a jolly break, Juliet. There's no need to be continually lip-locked, hands in back pockets, overly snuggled up in a manner that would embarrass Don Juan. Take a breather, at least long enough to knock back a glass of this sleepy number, put together with genuine, dry, *frizzante* Lambrusco from Italy (don't get suckered into the still variety, or—gasp—the American variety) and some other choice players. Even if you only stop the amore long enough to take a sip or three, at least you'll be able to get back at it in a more fortified manner.   SERVES 2

4 PEACH SLICES

½ OUNCE FRESHLY SQUEEZED LEMON JUICE

ICE CUBES

3 OUNCES CALVADOS

1½ OUNCES APRICOT BRANDY

4 DASHES ORANGE BITTERS

CHILLED LAMBRUSCO

1   *Place the peach slices and lemon juice into a cocktail shaker. Using a muddler or leftover arrow from Cupid's quiver, muddle well.*

2   *Fill the shaker halfway full with ice cubes. Add the Calvados, apricot brandy, and orange bitters. Shake well.*

3   *Strain the mixture into two flutes. Fill each glass with Lambrusco. Serve immediately.*

A NOTE: Feel this is too naked without a garnish even for your revelries? Then I suggest you add a couple more peach slices to the ingredients list, and use them wisely.

TROPICALIANA

Some days (such as those dreary days of nascent December or late February, when it seems the sun has fled forever), you feel like raising your hands to the sky and screaming, "I'm not taking it anymore!" The way around it isn't to lose your voice in pointless screaming (the weather doesn't take orders from us) or to indulge in listless moping. The way around it is to rewrite the story of that particular day. Remember, you're the author of your own life, by and large, so turn a desolate day into tropical bliss by filling the bathtub with sand (or half sand and half warm water), plugging a heat lamp into the bathroom fixture, suiting up in a swimsuit, mixing up one (or two) of these friendly drinks, and relaxing the day away in your self-created paradise. I'll bet you'll forget about any bleakness outside your door.   SERVES 2

ICE CUBES

2 OUNCES WHITE RUM

1 OUNCE DOMAINE DE CANTON GINGER LIQUEUR *(see A Note)*

1 OUNCE SIMPLE SYRUP *(page 16)*

½ OUNCE FRESHLY SQUEEZED LIME JUICE

CHILLED ROSÉ SPARKLING WINE

2 LIME SLICES *for garnish*

1   *Fill a cocktail shaker halfway full with ice cubes. Add the rum, ginger liqueur, simple syrup, and lime juice. Shake well.*

2   *Strain the mixture into two flute glasses. Top each with the rosé sparkling wine. Garnish each with a lime slice and serve.*

. . . .

A NOTE: Domaine de Canton Ginger Liqueur is made with fresh baby Vietnamese ginger, which is peeled and cut by hand, combined with herbs, spices, and honey, and then blended with eau de vie and VSOP and XO Grande Champagne cognacs, all in small batches. The end result is a bright ginger taste backed by an herbal, light sweetness that packs a bit of punch.

TIP TOP

You may consider, for a moment, that it's the brut sparkling wine that gives this fancy dancer its special élan, or you may judge that the wine's old pal brandy is the lead player in this performance, or you may regard, religiously, the Benedictine as the foremost spirit of the ingredient list. I, however, am giving the props right here and now to the dollop of fresh lemon juice. It's what brings every other ingredient together, while adding its own inimitable tang.   SERVES 2

ICE CUBES

3 OUNCES BRANDY

1 OUNCE BENEDICTINE

1 OUNCE FRESHLY SQUEEZED LEMON JUICE

1 OUNCE SIMPLE SYRUP *(page 16)*

CHILLED BRUT SEKT *or other sparkling wine*

1   *Fill a cocktail shaker halfway full with ice cubes. Add the brandy, Benedictine, lemon juice, and simple syrup. Shake well.*

2   *Fill two highball glasses halfway full with ice cubes. Strain the mixture into the glasses.*

3   *Slowly fill each glass with sparkling wine. Stir briefly.*

4

Around the WORLD on a Bubble

TRAINS, BALLOONS, PLANES, BOATS, CAMELS, horses, dogsleds, cars, trucks, buses, motorcycles, scooters, bicycles, pogo sticks, and feet are all good ways to travel the world. Actually riding a bubble is not a good way, but traveling the world of cross-continental cocktails and drinks that populate this chapter, which you can even do from your own backyard, might just be the most entertaining (and the cheapest) way to go from pole to pole. If you are actually traveling the world, and trying these drinks as you go? That's a truly fantastic trip.

CLASS OF
THE RACE

And they're off! Coming round the first corner, it looks like Kentucky bourbon has taken the lead, but then, into the second curve, Italian liqueur Benedictine is making its run. But what's this? A burst of speed into the third furlong and simple syrup jumps into the fray, with New Orleans's favorite pharmaceutical son Peychaud's bitters nipping at the heels. Wait just a minute, though, as they approach the finish line, from out of nowhere, French Champagne rears its regal head. It looks to be a photo finish, party fans. The flags are flying, and the winner is? Well, the winner is you, of course, because you get to enjoy this globe-trotting trotter. **SERVES 2**

ICE CUBES

4 OUNCES BOURBON

2 OUNCE BENEDICTINE

1 OUNCE SIMPLE SYRUP *(page 16)*

4 DASHES PEYCHAUD'S BITTERS

CHILLED BRUT CHAMPAGNE *(see A Note)*

1   *Fill a cocktail shaker halfway full with ice cubes. Add the bourbon, Benedictine, simple syrup, and bitters. Shake well, but not at a full gallop.*

2   *Strain the mixture into two flute glasses, and then top each with Champagne. Serve immediately.*

. . . .

A NOTE: To me, to go with all the class in this drink, real Champagne is needed.

BLUE TRAIN

Not the Blue Train Cocktail of Harry Craddock, author of the super *Savoy Cocktail Book* (1930), made up in the 1930s with blue vegetable extract (and which is sometimes seen today made with gin, blue curaçao, and lemon juice), this mix is a version of the Blue Train Special, which I first saw in Trader Vic's 1947 *Bartender's Guide*. And don't be fooled: Even though the name has "blue" in it, this is a drink for celebrations and fox-trotting, due to its effervescent nature (one of the many differences between it and Craddock's version).　SERVES 2

ICE CUBES

3 OUNCES BRANDY

2 OUNCES FRESH PINEAPPLE JUICE

CHILLED CAP CLASSIQUE *or other brut sparkling wine (see A Note)*

2 PINEAPPLE CHUNKS *for garnish (optional)*

1　*Fill a cocktail shaker three-quarters full with ice cubes. Add the brandy and pineapple juice. Shake well, and happily.*

2　*Strain the mixture into two flute glasses. Top each with chilled Cap Classique and garnish each with a pineapple chunk on a toothpick, if you need the extra snack. Serve immediately.*

A NOTE: Cap Classique is a South African sparkling wine made according to the traditional *méthode champenoise*, which works nicely if you can find it—and not just because there's an actual Blue Train that travels through that country.

EDEN

It may be that this slightly tropical, completely lovely hip-shaker should be enjoyed when the sun's in almost complete control—it's not uncomfortably hot, but neither is there a cloud in that big old sky. The Eden is refreshing, and it may make you want to lounge around in as few clothes as possible (original Eden-style). But let me play devil's advocate for just a sec, and say that I think the Eden is also ideal when the weather's the opposite of cuddly: cold, blustery, and downright icky. If you have an Eden in these circumstances, you'll be transported, at least for the time it takes to drink it, to a paradise, taking you away from the gray day. And isn't that a wonderful thing for a drink to do? I think John Milton would agree with me; after all, as he says in *Paradise Regained*, "And *Eden* rais'd in the wast Wilderness." If you can't *be* in paradise all the time, you might as well conjure up a little.

SERVES 4

ICE CUBES

8 OUNCES WHITE RUM

4 OUNCES CAMPARI

4 OUNCES FRESH PINEAPPLE JUICE

4 OUNCES FRESHLY SQUEEZED ORANGE JUICE

CHILLED PROSECCO

4 ORANGE SLICES *for garnish*

1   *Fill four highball glasses three-quarters full with ice cubes. Add 2 ounces rum, 1 ounce Campari, 1 ounce pineapple juice, and 1 ounce orange juice to each glass. Stir briefly.*

2   *Top each glass with Prosecco. Stir one more time. Garnish each with an orange slice and serve.*

IBF PICK-ME-UP

This is one that you must consume with friends. I repeat, must. The recipe's from a bouncing book called *Barflies and Cocktails*, by Harry and Wynn (Harry McElhone, proprietor of Harry's New York Bar in Paris, and caricaturist Wynn Holcomb, "with contributions by Arthur Moss," as the book tells us), which was originally published in 1927 but reprinted in 2008 by Mud Puddle Books. It has a host of classic recipes, some goofily wonderful drawings, and a whole lot of talk having to do with the International Bar Flies, or IBF, including specific recipes from its members (known historical names and others), folks who hung out and drank at the bar. And this communal spirit is why you must never drink this particular elixir alone.   SERVES 2

ICE CUBES

3 OUNCES BRANDY

1 OUNCE ORANGE CURAÇAO

1 OUNCE FERNET-BRANCA *(see A Note)*

CHILLED BRUT SPARKLING WINE

1   *Fill a cocktail shaker halfway full with ice cubes. Add the brandy, orange curaçao, and Fernet-Branca. Shake well.*

2   *Strain into two white wine glasses. Top each (almost to the top) with sparkling wine. Serve immediately.*

A NOTE: Fernet-Branca is an Italian amaro or bitter—the most bitter of the amaro family, as a matter of fact. It's been consumed and loved since 1835, and it contains a secret list of 27 ingredients (herbs and the like). Don't fear it, and you may just end up on the list of those who love it.

LAVANDA

Doesn't this sound like a risqué dance that's only mentioned in heated whispers along the back walls of respected waltz ballrooms? Before the main waltzers decide to take it to the streets, that is, slipping out of their upright façades (and limiting buttoned-up clothing) to embrace the sensuality of the Lavanda in a Lavanda dance-off against those shady (but cute) across-the-tracks dancers. Whew, all this hip-shaking is enough to make anyone thirsty. May I suggest the real Lavanda as a quencher? SERVES 2

4 LAVENDER SPRIGS

3 OUNCES GIN

1½ OUNCES LAVENDER SIMPLE SYRUP *(see A Note)*

ICE CUBES

CHILLED PROSECCO

1   *Place the flowers from two lavender sprigs, the gin, and the lavender simple syrup in a cocktail shaker. Using a muddler or wooden spoon, muddle well.*

2   *Fill the cocktail shaker halfway full with ice cubes. Shake like a dancer.*

3   *Strain into two flute glasses. Top each with chilled Prosecco, and garnish each with a lavender sprig. Serve immediately.*

A NOTE: To make lavender simple syrup, place ¼ cup chopped fresh lavender, 2 cups sugar, and 1½ cups water in a medium-sized saucepan. Heat over medium-high heat, stirring regularly, until it reaches a low boil. Once it reaches that low boil, reduce the heat to medium-low and keep the syrup at a simmer, still stirring, for 5 minutes. Remove from the heat and let cool completely. This makes about 3 cups. You can cut these measurements in half to make a smaller amount.

A SECOND NOTE: I originally created this recipe for the magazine *Every Day with Rachael Ray*, for an article on floral cocktails. If you need to serve this surrounded by blooms, as opposed to dancers, so be it.

JITTER SAUCE

Affable, boozy, incredibly readable, witty, and tipsy, British author Kingsley Amis wrote novels, poetry, short stories, and essays about drinking and a host of other subjects, and drank, from what I can tell, every conceivable liquor and liqueur under the clouds and sun. A recently released collection, *Everyday Drinking* (Bloomsbury, 2008), puts his three drinks books together in one volume, which is a boon for everyone who likes to drink and read (sometimes at the same time). I modified the following recipe from one found within its pages, and it's a stiff mix, not for the faint of heart—but some days demand such a drink. According to Mr. Amis, it was "popular in some circles at Oxford in the late thirties." **SERVES 2**

ICE CUBES

3 OUNCES GIN

2 OUNCES SCOTCH *(see A Note)*

CHILLED BRUT SPARKLING WINE

1   *Fill a cocktail shaker halfway full with ice cubes. Add the gin and Scotch. Stir well.*

2   *Strain into two flute glasses, top each with sparkling wine, and give a toast to all the good drink writers in this world and the world beyond.*

....

A NOTE: I suggest an easygoing blended Scotch here.

A SECOND NOTE: If you feel it's naked without it, slip a lemon twist in for garnish.

"*If you want to be a jitterbug, / First thing you do is git a mug; / Pour whisky, gin and wine within, / and then begin.*" —CAB CALLOWAY, AS QUOTED IN KINGSLEY AMIS'S *EVERYDAY DRINKING*, 2008

THE SEA HORSE

Though it won't whinny, and, for that matter, can't swim, the effervescent Sea Horse does have one thing in common with its natural namesake. They both serve as badges of eternal friendship (in traditional Hawaiian culture the marine version symbolizes this very idea). Which is why you should have those closest to you over this Friday and serve up a round (or two, or even three) of these, toast each other, give some hugs, and generally celebrate the fact that having great friends makes the world a better place. Since this uses the more-frequently-seen-but-still-not-everywhere sparkling Shiraz, from Australia, if you have to wait until the Friday after next (after you order a bottle online), not a one of them will hold it against you.   SERVES 4

ICE CUBES

6 OUNCES BRANDY

4 OUNCES FRESHLY SQUEEZED LEMON JUICE

8 DASHES ORANGE BITTERS *(see A Note)*

1 BOTTLE CHILLED SPARKLING SHIRAZ

1   *Fill a cocktail shaker halfway full with ice cubes. Add the brandy, lemon juice, and bitters. Shake well.*

2   *Strain the half-horse into four flute glasses. Top each with sparkling Shiraz. Stir briefly, and then serve.*

A NOTE: I suggest Regan's Orange Bitters No. 6 here—and to keep those friendships eternal, please go with my suggestion.

PENSIERO

Don't get down about it, but think about this for a moment (and think about the fact that *pensiero* means "thought" in Italian, too): In the world of sparkling wines, there are probably varieties, worthy varieties, you haven't yet tried. I know it's true for me. For example, until recently I'd missed out on Brachetto d'Acqui—and I'm something of an Italian nut (in the good way). Picking up its name from the Brachetto grape combined with the Acqui district in Italy's Piedmont region, this lightly fizzy number has a taste redolent of berries, cherries, spices, and flowers and is a bit sweet, making it an after-dinner partner of choice for many. It also works well with other ingredients, as in the Pensiero, which will help remind you that it's always good to be on the lookout for new liquid ideas. **SERVES 2**

ICE CUBES

2 OUNCES FRESHLY SQUEEZED ORANGE JUICE

1½ OUNCES PUNT E MES *(see A Note)*

1 OUNCE CAMPARI

1 OUNCE SIMPLE SYRUP *(page 16)*

CHILLED BRACHETTO D'ACQUI

2 LEMON TWISTS *for garnish*

1   *Fill a cocktail shaker halfway full with ice cubes. Add the orange juice, Punt e Mes, Campari, and simple syrup. Shake thoughtfully.*

2   *Strain the mixture into two flute glasses. Top each with Brachetto d'Acqui. Garnish each with a lemon twist and serve.*

A NOTE: Punt e Mes is an Italian vermouth, one that's a touch more bitter than others on the market (but not so bitter as to make you cringe). The name means "point and a half"; the story is that it comes from a corresponding rise in the stock market that gave a lucky investor enough proceeds to start the company.

VENETIAN SPRITZ

When traveling the world for sparkling cocktails, highballs, and drinks of all styles, you definitely want to make a stop in Italy. The well-deserved reputation of the Italian sparkler Prosecco and the enticements of lesser-known but still lovely bubblies such as Moscato d'Asti and Asti Spumante make it a must-visit. I believe, though, that it's also a key stop because of the Italian philosophy of *la dolce vita*, or the sweet life, a philosophy that espouses a relaxed state of being, where the focus is on enjoying life, food, and friends, and (perhaps best of all) on enjoying a tall, refreshing, transporting drink.   SERVES 4

ICE CUBES *(optional)*

6 OUNCES APEROL

CHILLED PROSECCO, *Moscato d'Asti, or Asti Spumante*

4 GREEN OLIVES (UNSTUFFED) *for garnish*

4 ORANGE SLICES OR WEDGES *for garnish*

1   *If the Prosecco isn't well chilled, or if you're feeling overheated or you want to have it as it would be served in Italy, place 1 or 2 ice cubes in each of four flute glasses. Add 1½ ounces Aperol to each flute.*

2   *Fill the glasses almost to the rim with Prosecco. Garnish each with an olive and an orange slice.*

SOME VARIATIONS: There are a number of variations you can play with when making a Spritz, corresponding to the wide variety of Italian liqueurs, the array of garnishing possibilities, and what you might actually be served in an Italian bar. For example, I always skip the olive (and if you order an Aperol Spritz in Italian bars outside of Venice, you are likely not to get one). Other ideas include a lemon twist on the above (my wife's favorite). Other liqueurs you might want to try in place of Aperol include Campari (with a lemon twist); Cynar, the artichoke liqueur (skipping the garnish); Strega, my favorite Italian liqueur; or limoncello, perhaps the most revered Italian liqueur of all.

LAMB'S WOOL

I had this first with Portland pals Katie and Ed, who are Italian Lambrusco freaks (a tag being assigned to more and more people) and with whom I've actually gone to Italy, staying in a little villa on the top of a hill that rests right on the border between Tuscany and Umbria (if that sounds dreamy to you, and it should, check out www.amicivillas.com). The reason all this goes together? Because the featured player here, Lambrusco, is an Italian red wine that is made in both sparkling and still versions. Be sure you get the real thing (and I mean the Italian *frizzante* one), because you do sometimes see the name on bottles that aren't Italian or aren't full of the bubbling nature that accompanies frolicking with fine friends so fantastically.   SERVES 2

ICE CUBES

3 OUNCES GIN

1 OUNCE DRY VERMOUTH

1 OUNCE TRIPLE SEC

CHILLED LAMBRUSCO

2 ORANGE SLICES *for garnish*

1   *Fill a cocktail shaker halfway full with ice cubes. Add the gin, dry vermouth, and triple sec. Shake well.*

2   *Strain into two flute glasses and top with the Lambrusco. Garnish each with an orange slice and serve.*

"Then he uncorked the bottle of red Lambrusco wine. The sick man ate and drank deliberately, not in order to prolong any gluttonous enjoyment but simply to get the full savor of his native earth. For you must realize that Lambrusco is no ordinary wine but something unique and particular to that section of the river valley."
—GIOVANNI GUARESCHI, *DON CAMILLO'S DILEMMA*, 1954

CHIARO DE LUNA

This romantic combination (with its sensual flavor mingling, its lovely Italian name that rolls off the tongue, and its allusion to moonlight, the favored lighting of most true romantics) comes from the King himself, Dale DeGroff. It shows its face within the pages of his *The Essential Cocktail* (Clarkson Potter, 2008), a book bursting with good recipes, good advice, and good tales and stories. Of course, when serving this up on a moonlit night, you may not want to actually open Mr. DeGroff's book—there's no reason to get derailed from the matter at hand. I'm sure he'd understand.   SERVES 2

6 PINEAPPLE CHUNKS

2 ROSEMARY SPRIGS

1 OUNCE ORGEAT SYRUP *(see A Note)*

8 OUNCES CHILLED PROSECCO

1   *Place 4 pineapple chunks, 1 rosemary sprig, and the orgeat into a mixing glass or cocktail shaker. Using a muddler or wooden spoon (a muddler's far more romantic, though), muddle well.*

2   *Carefully pour in the Prosecco. Using a long spoon, gently pull the ingredients from the bottom up, and then give a gentle stir.*

3   *Strain the mixture into two flute glasses (chilled, if possible, as Mr. DeGroff suggests). Garnish each with one of the remaining pineapple chunks and half of the remaining rosemary sprig. Serve immediately.*

A NOTE: Orgeat is an almond-flavored syrup that you can find in gourmet food stores and online.

5

The Freshest Effervescent MIXES

TRYING NEW THINGS MAY MAKE YOU SHIVER IN
fright, may make you a smidge nervous, or may make you excited
enough to jump out of your shoes. Whichever camp you stand within,
though, let me assure you that the following recipes, a selection of
new or newish sparkling drinks, are only going to make you ecstatic,
with their refreshing natures, interesting and well-balanced flavors,
and perfect-for-parties pleasantness. Which brings up a second dandy
point: Introducing your pals to these fresh mixes makes both you and
them happy—the ideal new situation.

THE AURORA COCKTAIL

It's so, so fun to go to a bar where the bartender is knowledgeable, can really shake it up, and makes drinks that transport you to a higher plane of existence (if I may be so bold). What happens, though, when a bar isn't reaching those levels? Well, they can call up someone (not that there are many others like him, really) such as the Cocktail Whisperer, Jamie Boudreau. One of the finest bartenders on the planet, Jamie can shake, strain, slice, twist, flame, and muddle with the best, and he can teach others—which is why he can fix up those bars that need it and also why you can catch his teaching videos, Raising the Bar, online at the Small Screen Network. Check out his helpful and pretty blog, Spirits and Cocktails, at spiritsandcocktails.wordpress.com, for tips and techniques as well as recipes. It's where I found the Aurora Cocktail, and my life's been better ever since. SERVES 2

½ OUNCE ABSINTHE

ICE CUBES

2 OUNCES COGNAC

2 OUNCES RYE

½ OUNCE ST-GERMAIN ELDERFLOWER LIQUEUR

2 DASHES SIMPLE SYRUP *(page 16)*

2 DASHES BOKER'S BITTERS *(see A Note)*

CHILLED BRUT CHAMPAGNE

2 LEMON TWISTS *for garnish*

1   *Place ¼ ounce absinthe in each of two cocktail or coupe glasses. Swirl within the glasses until the insides are completely covered, and then discard any remaining absinthe.*

2   *Fill a mixing glass halfway full with ice cubes. Add the Cognac, rye, St-Germain, simple syrup, and bitters. Stir well.*

3   *Strain the mixture into the glasses. Top each with a solid splash of Champagne. Garnish each with a lemon twist and serve.*

A NOTE: Boker's Bitters used to be on the bitters menu at every bar. Sadly, it faded from use and shelves. But luckily, Jamie has a recipe for it on his site (he's also a cocktail detective). If you decide not to make your own (it's lots of fun, though, so why not give it a go?), you can substitute Angostura bitters.

A SECOND NOTE: Not feeling the twist? Jamie says it's okay to use a cherry garnish, too.

"As to them, the man who can dream such iced champagne, such claret, port, or sherry, had better go to bed and stop there."
—CHARLES DICKENS, *MARTIN CHUZZLEWIT*, 1844

THE CAN CAN

Wow, what a day it is to be alive. It's now possible to get a whole truck-ful of different types of cocktail ingredients from all over the world. But that whole world of ingredients wouldn't be nearly as enjoyable if it weren't accompanied by the modern bar masters who are finding creative ways to combine said ingredients, with end results that tanta-lize, mesmerize, and make your parties out-of-sight—bar masters such as the lasses of LUPEC Boston, who are responsible for this very drink. LUPEC is an international association (it stands for Ladies United for the Preservation of Endangered Cocktails, and if there's a better acronym I haven't heard it), but the Boston branch is extra-active, with a must-read blog at www.lupecboston.com and cocktails, fundraisers, and enough fun to fill many, many cocktail shakers. SERVES 2

10 FRESH SOUR CHERRIES

2 OUNCES YELLOW CHARTREUSE

½ OUNCE FRESHLY SQUEEZED GRAPEFRUIT JUICE

2 DASHES ANGOSTURA BITTERS

ICE CUBES

CHILLED PROSECCO, *preferably Nino Franco (see A Note)*

1   *Place the sour cherries in a mixing glass or cocktail shaker. Using a muddler or sturdy wooden spoon, muddle those cherries well.*

2   *Add the Chartreuse, grapefruit juice, bitters, and ice cubes. Shake well, and strain the mixture into two flute glasses. Top each glass off with Prosecco, and serve.*

A NOTE: Nino Franco Prosecco is a nice affordable sparkler, one that has a light, frothy nature that pairs up perfectly here. If you can't find it at your local shop, try online at www.internetwines.com or another spot. You'll be happy you did.

"Kick up your heels and enjoy!" —LUPEC BOSTON

CAPRESE COCKTAIL

There are many innovative and inventive drinks out there. One new area that's being researched is molecular mixology—basically, influencing drink ingredients on a chemical level to create really intriguing mixes. Between us, sometimes they can be silly. But occasionally, they can taste amazing. One bartender who's not afraid to experiment but who also knows and reveres his classics is Andrew Wolfgang Bohrer, who writes the Cask Strength blog (www.caskstrength.wordpress.com) and who at this writing manages the bar at Seattle's Mistral. For this recipe, approximating the beloved Italian *insalata caprese*, Andrew accents Prosecco with homemade balsamic and tomato "caviar." And if that sentence made you, like me, say "wow," remember this: Even though it takes a little work to make, this cocktail is a showstopper.

SERVES 4

4 OUNCES BALSAMIC VINEGAR

2 OUNCES SIMPLE SYRUP *(page 16)*

2 OUNCES WATER

4 GRAMS SODIUM ALGINATE *(see A Note)*

7 OUNCES KETCHUP

1 OUNCE DEMITRI'S BLOODY MARY SEASONING *(see A Note)*

2 DASHES ANGOSTURA BITTERS

CALCIUM CHLORIDE *(see A Note)*

CHILLED PROSECCO

1 *Place the vinegar, simple syrup, and water in a medium-size bowl. Add half of the sodium alginate, and blend it in with an immersion blender or handheld mixer until it's completely combined, approximately 5 minutes.*

2 *Place the ketchup, Bloody Mary seasoning, and bitters in a mixing bowl. Mix briefly. Add the remaining sodium alginate, and blend it in with an immersion blender or handheld mixer until it's completely combined, about 5 minutes more.*

3 *Fill one squeeze bottle with the balsamic gel and one squeeze bottle with the tomato gel, and refrigerate for 24 hours.*

4 *Create a calcium chloride bath in a mixing bowl by combining 2 parts calcium chloride to 98 parts water by weight. Drop tiny drops from the squeeze bottles into the bath (see A Second Note). Once you've gone through the bottles' contents, strain the "caviar" from the bath and rinse carefully in water.*

5 *Add a little of the "caviar" to each of 4 flutes. Top with Prosecco and serve immediately.*

. . . .

A NOTE: Having problems finding Demitri's Bloody Mary Seasoning? Try online at www.demitris.com. Sodium alginate and calcium chloride are easily found online—try Google shopping for a few choices, but just be sure you order food-grade versions.

A SECOND NOTE: If you'd like, place a strainer over the bowl so it's sitting in the liquid—that way, you won't have to pour the "caviar" into a strainer.

A THIRD NOTE: To make this truly echo the caprese salad experience, serve the drink alongside fresh buffalo mozzarella topped with basil chiffonade and cracked black pepper.

ESTEEM

Hey, you're all right. Really, I think you're pretty darn swell, and I'm sure I'm not the only one. I mean, I don't want you to get all self-help-y here, nor do I want you to stop striving for greatness (and I definitely want you to *keep* striving for greater parties), but hey, why not give yourself a pat on the back? You've done a heck of a job so far. And for that matter, I suggest making yourself one of these beauties as a vibrant and flavorful means of self-celebration.   SERVES 2

ICE CUBES

3 OUNCES GIN

1 OUNCE ANISETTE *(see A Note)*

1 OUNCE FRESHLY SQUEEZED LIME JUICE

CHILLED BRUT CHAMPAGNE *(see A Second Note)*

1   *Fill a cocktail shaker halfway full with ice cubes. Add the gin, anisette, and lime juice. Shake while smiling.*

2   *Strain into two flute glasses and fill each almost to the rim with chilled Champagne. Serve immediately.*

. . . .

A NOTE: Anisette is, as you might guess, an anise-flavored liqueur, one that's a bit sweet and that you should be able to find at your local liquor store. Or check online.

A SECOND NOTE: I think using real Champagne is best here—because you deserve it.

SHAKING PANSY

When browsing drinks booklets (such as the *Calvert Party Encyclopedia*, put out by the Calvert Distillery back in 1960) and books (such as Trader Vic's *Bartender's Guide* and Patrick Gavin Duffy's *Official Mixer's Manual*), I've seen a few recipes for the Pansy, a fairly straightforward cocktail with absinthe, grenadine, and bitters, the consumption of two or three of which would, I think, turn any pansy into less mouse and more lion. Perhaps the Pansy was even responsible for a number of relationships, maybe even marriages, during the early part of the last century, when it was probably more in vogue. And because of that, I'm strongly for it (it tastes swell, too). But I think if you really want to go from milksop to man about town or from wallflower to glamour girl, you should have some Champagne or sparkling wine in your drink as well, to class things up. SERVES 4

ICE CUBES

6 OUNCES ABSINTHE

2 OUNCES GRENADINE

8 DASHES ANGOSTURA BITTERS

CHILLED CAVA *or other sparkling wine (see A Note)*

1 *Fill a cocktail shaker halfway full with ice cubes. Add the absinthe, grenadine, and bitters. Shake strongly.*

2 *Strain the mixture into four very attractive flute glasses. Top each with Cava. Serve immediately.*

A NOTE: I like the Cava-style sparkling wine in this to get the shaking going right. But if you want to use another brut sparkler, I won't fight it.

SBAGLIATO

This Italian fix may not be fresh to those actually residing in Italy, but it was fresh to me, and so fits in with the other fresh faces in this chapter. I heard of it when staying in Florence (ah, Florence—art, food, amiable folks, pals Emanuele, Caterina, and Emiliano . . . just typing the city's name sends me into a reverie) at the Hotel Casci, a handy spot just blocks from the Duomo. Where it goes above and beyond "handy" is in the little bar (and isn't it wonderful how Italian hotels have little bars in them—not fancy, overdone numbers, but simple bars with good liqueurs and the basics and a couple of stools or small tables?) and bartender and counterman Pierre, who served me this drink, which is a basic variation on the classic Negroni, with sparkling wine instead of gin. Funnily enough, *sbagliato* means "wrong," but the taste of this drink is more than right.   SERVES 2

ICE CUBES

3 OUNCES SWEET VERMOUTH

3 OUNCES CAMPARI

CHILLED BRUT SPARKLING WINE

2 ORANGE TWISTS *for garnish*

1   *Fill a cocktail shaker halfway full with ice cubes. Add the vermouth and Campari. Shake well.*

2   *Strain the mixture into two flute glasses. Top with the sparkling wine and garnish each glass with an orange twist.*

A NOTE: I could see the rationale behind serving this in a cocktail glass in the Negroni's honor. I could also see the rationale behind calling this a sparkling Americano. But it doesn't mean I'm going to do either of them.

A VARIATION: You could use the Italian sparkling wines Prosecco, Moscato d'Asti, or Asti Spumante here and be happy about it.

THE VERY VERNALAGNIA

Sure, spring is oodles of oozing *muy divertido*, with the newly uncovered sun (not to mention the newly uncovered calves that sun brings out), the freshly alive feeling everyone seems to have after the long winter, the blooming flowers everywhere, and the people whistling and winking and generally overflowing with happiness. . . . It's almost enough to leave one breathless. This Spanish-influenced mingler matches up with that seasonal breathlessness, but it also balances out the happy madness, thanks to its refreshing nature. Because of this duality, it's a good partner for those spring days.   SERVES 2

ICE CUBES

2 OUNCES BRANDY

1 OUNCE ANISETTE

4 DASHES BITTERMENS XOCOLATL MOLE BITTERS

8 OUNCES CHILLED CAVA

2 LEMON WHEELS *for garnish (optional)*

1   *Fill a mixing glass halfway full with ice cubes. Add the brandy, anisette, and bitters. Using a long spoon, stir well.*

2   *Strain equally into two flute glasses. Top each with 4 ounces Cava, and garnish with a lemon wheel if desired. Serve immediately.*

A NOTE: Cava is a Spanish sparkling wine made since 1872 in the traditional method. It comes in white or rosé. For this recipe, I tend toward the former but won't hold you back from trying the latter.

TEMPORARY GETAWAY

Admit it: Some afternoons would be nicer spent traveling through Europe. Of course, responsibilities keep the dream from translating into reality every ol' afternoon when we want to be saying *oui oui* or *ja ja* to another drink instead of "Be there in a minute" when summoned to the next meeting. On those days when you have to stay in place, turn your mood around a touch with a Temporary Getaway. Its mingling of fresh juices, the French elderflower liqueur St-Germain, and the German sparkling wine Sekt is sure to transport you.   SERVES 2

8 APPLE SLICES

1 OUNCE FRESHLY SQUEEZED ORANGE JUICE

½ OUNCE FRESHLY SQUEEZED LEMON JUICE

ICE CUBES

2 OUNCES ST-GERMAIN ELDERFLOWER LIQUEUR

8 OUNCES CHILLED BRUT SEKT *(see A Note)*

1   *Place 6 apple slices, the orange juice, and the lemon juice in a cocktail shaker or mixing glass. Using a muddler or wooden spoon, muddle well.*

2   *Fill the cocktail shaker halfway full with ice cubes. Add the St-Germain, and, using a long spoon, stir well.*

3   *Pour the chilled Sekt into the cocktail shaker or glass. Stir briefly, being sure to bring up the fruit on the bottom when stirring.*

4   *Strain into two flutes or cocktail/coupe glasses (I like the way the latter breathes, but a flute's more traditional). Garnish with the remaining apple slices (putting a little notch in if needed for rim balancing) and serve.*

A NOTE: You could use another sparkling wine here, but it wouldn't be the same (and not only because Sekt tends to be a smidge on the sweeter side). Look for a bottle labeled *Deutscher Sekt*, which means only German grapes were used. If you can't find one, try to substitute a different German sparkling wine.

BUBBLY POINSETTIA

I originally created this both for a holiday cocktail class at Seattle's Dish It Up, a kitchen products store, wine shop, and classroom rolled up deliciously into one space (check out www.dish-it-up.com for more), and for an article in *Traditional Home* magazine about the class. Needless to say, it's a seasonal favorite (if the name didn't give it away, the coloring would), and it works wonderfully if you want to take your holiday happening a step above the ordinary. SERVES 2

ICE CUBES

3 OUNCES GIN

1½ OUNCES GRENADINE *(see A Note)*

1 OUNCE MARASCHINO LIQUEUR

½ OUNCE FRESHLY SQUEEZED LEMON JUICE

CHILLED BRUT CHAMPAGNE *or sparkling wine*

2 LEMON SLICES *for garnish (optional)*

1   *Fill a cocktail shaker halfway full with ice cubes. Add the gin, grenadine, maraschino liqueur, and lemon juice. Shake jollily.*

2   *Strain the mixture into two flute glasses. Top each with chilled Champagne. Garnish each with a lemon slice if you're wearing a holiday hat (or at least want your drink to have a headpiece). Serve immediately.*

....

A NOTE: If you're buying grenadine (and, like most of us, haven't yet taken to making your own), I suggest either the Scrappy's or the Stirrings brand. Both are not as sickly sweet as what's normally found on store shelves and have much better flavor. Look for them online.

HOW2HEROES SPARKLER

If this title doesn't seem effusive enough for a celebratory quaff of this magnitude, then I suggest rolling out its longer moniker, the How-2Heroes Anniversario Celebratorio Special Sparkler. Too long? Then how about the quick-fire Heroic Sparkler? Whichever you go with on your gala invite, remember that this was created to toast the first anniversary of the food- and drink-video website How2Heroes.com, a site I suggest visiting if you're into eating, drinking, or having fun (or a combination of the above, like most right-minded folks). The site has oodles of helpful videos, but you can also upload your own videos. I hope that when you do, you'll have a glass of this with you in the frame.

SERVES 2

2 KIWI WHEELS *(see A Note)*

2 LEMON SLICES

ICE CUBES

3 OUNCES GIN

1½ OUNCES ST-GERMAIN ELDERFLOWER LIQUEUR

4 DASHES ORANGE BITTERS

CHILLED BRUT SPARKLING WINE

1   *Place the kiwi and lemon slices in a cocktail shaker. Using a muddler or an anniversary pennant, muddle well.*

2   *Fill the cocktail shaker halfway full with ice cubes. Add the gin, St-Germain, and bitters. Shake well.*

3   *Strain the mixture into two flute glasses. Top each with sparkling wine. Stir gently, and then serve.*

A NOTE: When making kiwi wheels and slices, be sure you don't include the skin (unlike with a lemon slice, say), because it's yucky.

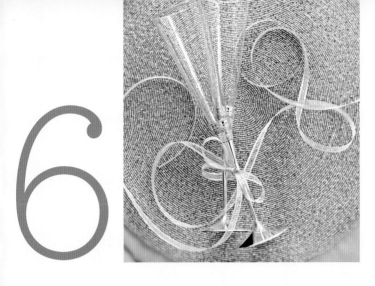

6

SPARKLERS
for Swarming
CROWDS

MAYBE YOU AREN'T HAVING YOUR WHOLE ADDRESS
book over for a springtime soirée, and maybe the whole extended family
isn't descending for this year's holiday reunion, but darn, it sure seems
like a large number of folks will be arriving, thirsty, before long. Here's
where sparkling punches like the Cardinal, Regent's Punch, the Storied
Life, and their siblings in this chapter become your closest compadres,
because their serve-a-bunch-at-once nature takes the pressure off. So you
actually get to kick back and laugh a lot at this year's party.

CARDINAL

This is kind of a curious punch, at first glance, with its two liquors, two kinds of bubbles, English drawing-room favorite claret (but no ascots to be found), and (as if that weren't enough) a curious coalescence of sweet vermouth, orange, pineapple, and a bit of simple syrup (well, maybe a touch more than a bit—a sweet bite, let's call it). It almost seems, at that first glance, doomed to fail. But to use a metaphor that matches the title, it flies like a bird, with every flavor slipping here and there to the forefront (like birds in a flock, as they fly), and with a serious undertone hiding within that allows it to both charm and fortify. As a bonus, it looks lovely, with a deep, rich coloring. All in all, it's so darn swell that I nominated it for Punch of the Year, 2008. And you know what? It won. Of course, I was the only judge, but hey, that's how the contest went. SERVES 10 TO 12

16 OUNCES CLARET

12 OUNCES BRANDY

12 OUNCES DARK RUM

12 OUNCES SIMPLE SYRUP *(page 16)*

4 OUNCES SWEET VERMOUTH

ICE ROUND *or cracked ice*

1 ORANGE, *cut into slices*

5 PINEAPPLE SLICES, *peeled and cut into chunks*

ONE 2-LITER BOTTLE CHILLED CLUB SODA

ONE 750-MILLILITER BOTTLE BRUT SPARKLING WINE

1   *Pour the claret, brandy, rum, simple syrup, and vermouth into a large punch bowl. Stir slightly with a long spoon.*

2   *Add the ice round to the punch, or add enough cracked ice that the bowl is almost halfway full.*

3   *Add the orange slices and pineapple chunks, and slowly add the club soda. Stir again, but not frantically.*

4   *Gently add the sparkling wine and stir—but just once more. Serve in white wine glasses or punch cups.*

THREE CATS

Never, ever, serve this meowing number at a mixer where dog aficionados are in attendance. It just won't go down. And never, ever, tell my two pooches (whom I love to death, but who have what I would call a very temperamental relationship with cats) that I gave you the recipe for this furry liquid friend—it's best they don't know I'm touting the cat family. And never, ever, actually give this to your cat, even if he or she is your best pal and wakes you up every morning with a smooch. Actually, you can forget the first point—instead, never serve this to anyone who doesn't like rum, 'cause it's rum-a-licious.   SERVES 10 TO 12

ONE 750-MILLILITER BOTTLE DARK RUM

18 OUNCES FRESH PINEAPPLE JUICE

12 OUNCES SIMPLE SYRUP *(page 16)*

4 OUNCES FRESHLY SQUEEZED LEMON JUICE

ICE BLOCK *or cracked ice*

ONE 750-MILLILITER BOTTLE CAP CLASSIQUE
or other brut sparkling wine (see A Note)

2 CUPS PINEAPPLE CHUNKS

2 CUPS SLICED STRAWBERRIES

1   *Place the rum, pineapple juice, simple syrup, and lemon juice in a punch bowl. Stir 12 times, with a long spoon, ladle, or cat o' nine tails. Add the ice to the punch bowl.*

2   *Pour the sparkling wine in creepingly, and then add the pineapple and strawberries. Stir 12 more times (in the opposite direction). Serve in punch cups, wine glasses, or little mugs with pictures of cute cats on them.*

A NOTE: Although Cap Classique, a South African sparkling wine made by the traditional *méthode champenoise*, goes well here, the cats won't cry too much if you have to sub in another sparkling wine.

A ROSE IS A ROSÉ

There's little in life more romantic than a bunch of roses, some sweet talk, some Commodores on the stereo, and about eight friends drinking out of the punch bowl. Okay, maybe that's not all that romantic. But hey, sometimes the best romances come out of parties with pals, and parties and punches go together oh-so-well, and, well, to be honest, a little liquid courage doesn't hurt on the romance front. Seen in that rosy light, maybe this situation is romantic. And, if nothing else, why not invite some single friends over, hand out the glasses brimming with this lovely mix, and play matchmaker? SERVES 8 TO 10

2 CUPS MARASCHINO CHERRIES *(see A Note)*

8 OUNCES GIN

8 OUNCES FRESHLY SQUEEZED ORANGE JUICE

6 OUNCES MARASCHINO LIQUEUR

6 OUNCES GRAND MARNIER

4 OUNCES GREEN CHARTREUSE

ICE BLOCK

ONE 750-MILLILITER BOTTLE CHILLED ROSÉ SPARKLING WINE

ONE 1-LITER BOTTLE CHILLED CLUB SODA

1   *Place the maraschino cherries, gin, orange juice, maraschino liqueur, Grand Marnier, and Chartreuse in a punch bowl. Stir slightly. Add the block of ice.*

2   *Pour the sparkling rosé and then the club soda into the bowl. Stir again. Serve in punch glasses or white wine glasses.*

A NOTE: If you can get them, I suggest using Tillen Farms Merry Maraschino cherries here (www.tillenfarms.com). Or go with fresh Rainier cherries and a splash of simple syrup (page 16).

CHAMPAGNE PUNCH

"Of course," you might roll out, in that petulant tone of voice used when still waiting for a drink but not having yet received one and so you are on the bitter side of testy—though who can blame you, as you've had a hard day dealing with those jerky people out there (who, it must be admitted, are also probably waiting for drinks now)—and here I am making Champagne Punch, leading you to say, again, "Of course, it's a little silly to call *this* Champagne Punch, when there are enough of them that you could fill a whole chapter easily." And I could tell you how this, to me, is the original sparkling punch, the one I was weaned on, and so deserves to stand alone in a small, bright spotlight. Instead, I'll just pour you a glass of the spirited stuff and we can move on into the happier evening.   SERVES 10

ICE BLOCK *or large chunks of ice*

6 OUNCES FRESHLY SQUEEZED ORANGE JUICE

2 OUNCES FRESHLY SQUEEZED LIME JUICE

2 OUNCES FRESHLY SQUEEZED LEMON JUICE

4 OUNCES SIMPLE SYRUP *(page 16)*

6 OUNCES LIGHT RUM

6 OUNCES DARK RUM

ONE 750-MILLILITER BOTTLE CHILLED BRUT CHAMPAGNE

ORANGE, LIME, AND LEMON SLICES

1   *Place the block of ice in a large punch bowl. If using chunks of ice, fill the bowl just under halfway full with them.*

2   *Add the juices and the simple syrup. With a long spoon, stir 10 times. Add the rums and then stir 10 more times.*

3   *Add the Champagne in a mellow manner, stir slightly, and then add a bunch of fruit slices.*

4   *Ladle into punch glasses or goblets to serve, and try (for goodness' sake) to get a bit of fruit in each glass.*

SAUCY

Quit giving me that lip (what us old folks call "the sauce"), you young whippersnapper, and get your hands off my glass of the Saucy. If you want your own glass, then you're gonna have to learn a little respect for your elders, those folks doddering off in the corner, saying that your take on drinking and laughing and enjoying this here party moment with a giggle and a song is, well, silly. Wait, wait, wait a minute. I don't wanna be doddering in the corner (and here's hoping you don't either). Take this glass of the Saucy, and I'll get one too, and then let's trade playful jabs and jokes. **SERVES 8**

6 PLUMS, *pitted and coarsely chopped*

4 OUNCES FRESHLY SQUEEZED LEMON JUICE

14 OUNCES GIN

6 OUNCES COINTREAU

12 DASHES PEYCHAUD'S BITTERS

ICE BLOCK, *cracked ice, or an ice ring*

ONE 750-MILLILITER BOTTLE CHILLED ROSÉ SPARKLING WINE

1   *Place the plums and lemon juice in a sturdy pitcher. Using a muddler or sturdy wooden spoon, muddle well.*

2   *Place a mesh strainer over a punch bowl. Pour the mixture through the strainer into the bowl. Let the juices drip out of the strainer for a minute, using the muddler or wooden spoon to push the juice through as needed.*

3   *Add the gin, Cointreau, and bitters to the bowl. Stir briefly.*

4   *Add the ice (filling about halfway if using cracked ice), and then the rosé sparkling wine. Stir again, smoothly and while smiling, and serve.*

> *"In this connection I feel I must deal with the problem of pink champagne. It is well known that many a romance has been wrecked for the lack of this romantic tipple."*
> —PAUL HOLT, "THE WINE AND THE WAISTCOAT,"
> *THE COMPLEAT IMBIBER, NO. 1,* 1956

HARVEST BOWL

Gather round the Harvest Bowl, holding partners by the hand, now swing to the left, now swing to the right, stir a few times, pour it up (and not too light), take a big sip, give a little bow, another little sip, a do-si-do, one more slight sip, grab your partner by the elbow, now promenade. And that's the Harvest Bowl shuffle (and it isn't square in the least). **SERVES 10**

ICE BLOCK *or cracked ice*

15 OUNCES APPLE CIDER

7½ OUNCES VODKA

5 OUNCES ORANGE CURAÇAO

1 APPLE, *sliced*

1 LEMON, *sliced*

ONE 750-MILLILITER BOTTLE CHILLED SPARKLING APPLE JUICE

ONE 750-MILLILITER BOTTLE CHILLED BRUT CHAMPAGNE
or sparkling wine (see A Note)

1   *Place the block of ice in a large punch bowl (if going with cracked ice, fill the bowl halfway).*

2   *Add the cider, vodka, curaçao, and apple and lemon slices. Using a long spoon or ladle, dance the ingredients a few times 'round.*

3   *Carefully add the sparkling apple juice and then the Champagne. Using that same long spoon or ladle, stir a few more times. Serve in wine glasses or goblets.*

A NOTE: You can go with another sparkling wine here, instead of Champagne, but not if your dance is in France. That would be frowned upon.

REGENT'S PUNCH

An erstwhile chum from the days when punches were more reliable and more often made by English gentlemen in darkly paneled rooms, this onetime classic appears in most venerable bar guides (including "The Professor" Jerry Thomas's *Bar-Tender's Guide*, in my 1887 version) as well as more modern cocktail books such as David Wondrich's *Imbibe!* (Perigee, 2007), which is about Mr. Thomas. See how everything works together? Much like a good punch. There are variations on the Regent's recipe a-poppin' then, as you might expect, but most have at least a handful of things in common: green tea, dark rum, lemon juice, a sweetening agent, brandy or Cognac, the addition of the bubbles before serving, and sometimes orange, pineapple, and other beauties. The version below gets you there and then some, and lets you feel like a king or queen stand-in, too (it is a drink for regents, after all). **SERVES 10 TO 12**

3 LEMONS

12 OUNCES FRESHLY SQUEEZED LEMON JUICE

10 OUNCES SIMPLE SYRUP *(page 16)*

16 OUNCES HOT GREEN TEA

12 OUNCES BRANDY *(see A Note)*

6 OUNCES DARK RUM *(see A Second Note)*

4 OUNCES ORANGE CURAÇAO

ICE BLOCK *or cracked ice*

TWO 750-MILLILITER BOTTLES CHILLED BRUT CHAMPAGNE

2 CUPS PINEAPPLE CHUNKS

2 ORANGES, *cut into slices*

1   *Wash and peel the lemons, working to get as little of the white pith as possible. Place the peels, lemon juice, and simple syrup in a large punch bowl that can stand the heat.*

2   *Pour the hot green tea into the punch bowl. Stir well, and let it cool.*

3   *Add the brandy, rum, and orange curaçao. Stir again, and let sit for a few minutes (you want to make sure it's cooled down).*

4   *Add that block of ice, or a goodly amount of cracked ice, and then pour the Champagne into the bowl, slowly and surely.*

5   *Add the fruit, stir, and serve immediately in punch cups or other regal glassware.*

....

A NOTE: If you don't mind ponying up for it, go with VSOP Cognac instead of brandy.

A SECOND NOTE: Using sturdy Jamaican rum is traditional and tasty, a genuinely enduring combination.

A THIRD NOTE: If you can find the elusive Batavia Arrack, then for gosh sakes, add about 6 ounces to this mixture. And then call me and have me over.

> "When the day arrived, my very carpet-bag was an object of veneration to the stipendiary clerks, to whom the house at Norwood was a sacred mystery. One of them informed me that he had heard that Mr. Spenlow ate entirely off plate and china; and another hinted at champagne being constantly on draught, after the usual custom of table beer."
> —CHARLES DICKENS, *DAVID COPPERFIELD*, 1850

THE SWEETER WELCOME

I'm not saying that everything would have been peachy if the witches three had been stirring up a big batch of this playful potion at the beginning of Shakespeare's *Macbeth* (though I am saying that I'm the first one to use the word "peachy" in relation to *Macbeth*), or that Duncan wouldn't have argued with his hasty general, or that Lady M wouldn't have been quite such a bloody social climber. I *am* of the mind that if they had shared a glass of this they would have held their hands in place a little longer and thought a little more about those daggers. And if sharing two glasses, maybe they would have just laughed and gone for a swim. It might not have been such a memorable play, but it would have been more fun. SERVES 8

1 LEMON

8 OUNCES GIN

8 OUNCES APEROL

4 OUNCES PUNT E MES

4 OUNCES FRESHLY SQUEEZED LEMON JUICE

ICE BLOCK (*or cracked ice, if you aren't afraid of witches' wrath*)

ONE 750-MILLILITER BOTTLE BRACHETTO D'ACQUI (*see A Note*)

1   *Carefully peel the lemon, working to get as little of the white pith as possible. Chop the peel into 1-inch pieces, and place it in a punch bowl.*

2   *Add the gin, Aperol, Punt e Mes, and lemon juice to the bowl. Stir, and let it memorize its lines for a few minutes.*

3   *Add the ice block to the bowl (or fill the bowl about halfway with cracked ice), and stir.*

4   *Add the Brachetto d'Acqui, stir once more, and serve in smallish medieval goblets, along with a disarming smile.*

A NOTE: Brachetto d'Acqui is an Italian red sparkling wine that's a whisper or two sweet and fruity.

STORIED LIFE

One of the best moments (maybe it would be better to say "the best series of moments," as I remember one such occasion that lasted for three days, but we were full of vim and vigor then) of any afternoon or evening spent relaxing around a table with, say, three or four boon companions is when the tales are spun. Once tongues are loosened, the yarns are told and told again. Remember that one time, and the bull that chased you across the field? Or that time you ended up winning 16 games of shuffleboard in a row? Or that time you woke up on a plane to Bermuda? If you have a punch bowl, and are heading toward an evening of stories and song, may I suggest the following punch as a participant? You may end up with even more stories the next day.
SERVES 6

CRACKED ICE

12 OUNCES BOURBON

6 OUNCES SWEET VERMOUTH

6 OUNCES FRESHLY SQUEEZED ORANGE JUICE

3 OUNCES CAMPARI

ONE 750-MILLILITER BOTTLE CHILLED PROSECCO

1 ORANGE, *sliced*

1   *Fill a punch bowl halfway full with cracked ice.*

2   *Add the bourbon, vermouth, orange juice, and Campari. Stir well with a long spoon or a pencil.*

3   *Pour in the Prosecco and add the orange slices. Stir again, briefly, and then serve in sturdy punch bowls or cups.*

"He was visibly mellow, as he had just come from a punch bowl,
which had been the subject of a wager at the club..."
—THEODOR FONTANE, *TRIALS AND TRIBULATIONS*, 1917

MEASUREMENT EQUIVALENTS

Please note that all conversions are approximate.

LIQUID CONVERSIONS

U.S.	IMPERIAL	METRIC
1 tsp	—	5 ml
1 tbs	$1/2$ fl oz	15 ml
2 tbs	1 fl oz	30 ml
3 tbs	$1^{1}/_2$ fl oz	45 ml
$1/4$ cup	2 fl oz	60 ml
$1/3$ cup	$2^{1}/_2$ fl oz	75 ml
$1/3$ cup + 1 tbs	3 fl oz	90 ml
$1/3$ cup + 2 tbs	$3^{1}/_2$ fl oz	100 ml
$1/2$ cup	4 fl oz	120 ml
$2/3$ cup	5 fl oz	150 ml
$3/4$ cup	6 fl oz	180 ml
$3/4$ cup + 2 tbs	7 fl oz	200 ml
1 cup	8 fl oz	240 ml
1 cup + 2 tbs	9 fl oz	275 ml
$1^{1}/_4$ cups	10 fl oz	300 ml
$1^{1}/_3$ cups	11 fl oz	325 ml
$1^{1}/_2$ cups	12 fl oz	350 ml
$1^{2}/_3$ cups	13 fl oz	375 ml
$1^{3}/_4$ cups	14 fl oz	400 ml
$1^{3}/_4$ cups + 2 tbs	15 fl oz	450 ml
2 cups (1 pint)	16 fl oz	475 ml
$2^{1}/_2$ cups	20 fl oz	600 ml
3 cups	24 fl oz	720 ml
4 cups (1 quart)	32 fl oz	945 ml

(1,000 ml is 1 liter)

INDEX

NOTE: Page references in *italics* indicate photographs.

ABOUT THE AUTHOR

A.J. Rathbun is the award-winning author of *Good Spirits, Dark Spirits, Wine Cocktails, Luscious Liqueurs, Party Drinks!, Party Snacks!,* and *Double Take* (coauthored with Jeremy Holt). As a loquacious expert on matters of food, drinks, and entertaining, Rathbun is a frequent guest on the Everyday Food program (Martha Stewart Living/Sirius satellite radio) and is a contributor to magazines such as *Every Day with Rachael Ray, The Food Network Magazine, Real Simple, Eating Well,* and *Wine Enthusiast,* among many others. Rathbun's popular cocktail classes at the Dish It Up cooking school in Seattle have been profiled in *Traditional Homes* magazine. He is a member of the International Association of Culinary Professionals and the Museum of the American Cocktail. A.J. lives in Seattle, and invites you to visit his website, www.ajrathbun.com, where you can read his blog, Spiked Punch.